1,000 AMAZING WEIRD FACTS

Penguin
Random
House

SECOND EDITION
DK Delhi
Senior editor Neha Ruth Samuel
Assistant art editor Diya Varma
Senior picture researcher Sumedha Chopra
Deputy managing editor Sreshtha Bhattacharya
Deputy managing art editor Shreya Anand
Managing editor Kingshuk Ghoshal
Managing art editor Govind Mittal
DTP designers Bimlesh Tiwari, Vikram Singh
Senior DTP designer Harish Aggarwal
Senior jackets coordinator Priyanka Sharma Saddi

DK London
Senior editor Shaila Brown **Senior art editor** Jacqui Swan
US Senior editor Jennette ElNaggar
US Executive editor Lori Cates Hand
Managing editor Rachel Fox
Managing art editor Owen Peyton Jones
Production editor Gillian Reid
Senior production controller Laura Andrews
Jacket designer Akiko Kato
Jacket design development manager Sophia MTT
Publisher Andrew Macintyre
Associate publishing director Liz Wheeler
Art director Karen Self
Publishing director Jonathan Metcalf

Fact checkers Steve Hoffman,
Priyanka Lamichhane, Michelle Rae Harris
Contributor Andrea Mills

Content previously published in *Strange But True!*

FIRST EDITION
Senior editor Victoria Pyke **Editor** Jenny Sich
Editorial assistant Charlie Galbraith
Senior designer Sheila Collins **Designer** David Ball
Managing editor Linda Esposito
Managing art editor Philip Letsu
Fact checking Hazel Beynon
Picture research Nic Dean, Sarah Smithies
Illustrator Stuart Jackson Carter
Jacket design Mark Cavanagh
Jacket design development manager Sophia MTT
Producer (pre-production) Nikoleta Parasaki
Acting senior producer Vivienne Yong
Publisher Andrew Macintyre **Art director** Karen Self
Associate publishing director Liz Wheeler
Publishing director Jonathan Metcalf

Author Andrea Mills

This American Edition, 2023
First American Edition, 2015
Published in the United States by DK Publishing
1745 Broadway, 20th Floor, New York, NY 10019

CONTENTS

1 WHAT ON EARTH?

What on Earth?

Weird and wonderful places abound on our planet. Fire, air, earth, and water combine to craft some of the most unforgettable places on Earth. From glistening glaciers and an island in the clouds to multicolored mountains and forests of stone, these extraordinary environments are out of this world.

Turkey's stunning blue pools at Pamukkale (meaning "cotton castle") are produced by the region's natural hot springs. Mineral-rich waters, which are said to have healing properties, build up in rock-pool terraces.

THE ORANGE
DOOR TO HELL

Welcome to **Hell on Earth**. More than 50 years ago, in the desert of Turkmenistan, workers drilling for gas got quite a fright when a **humongous hole** suddenly opened up. The resulting **crater of fire** still burns today, with locals naming the hot spot the "Door to Hell."

SUDDEN SINKHOLES

Sinkholes occur where supporting structures break down, most commonly in limestone areas. Water trickles underground, dissolving rock and creating caverns. When a cavern roof weakens, the ground opens, forming a sinkhole like this one in Guatemala.

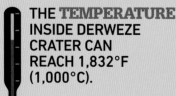
THE **TEMPERATURE** INSIDE DERWEZE CRATER CAN REACH 1,832°F (1,000°C).

VISITORS CAN SPEND THE NIGHT IN **YURTS** PITCHED UP BESIDE THE CRATER.

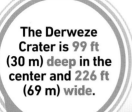

The **Derweze Crater is 99 ft (30 m) deep in the center and 226 ft (69 m) wide.**

Light produced by the burning gas is visible many miles away.

FAST FACTS

Sea sinkholes can occur in coastal areas. Water cuts through limestone to form caverns, into which the sinkhole collapses. If the cavern meets the sea, the level of the water in the hole rises and falls with the tide.

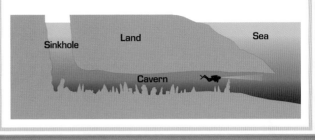

Sinkhole   Land   Sea
Cavern

It is believed that in 1971, drilling for gas in Derweze, Turkmenistan, went badly wrong when the ground collapsed and swallowed the drilling equipment. Workers set fire to the exposed gas reservoir to prevent poisonous gases from leaking out. They assumed the fire would burn out, but it still rages.

IN 2014, ADVENTURER GEORGE KOUROUNIS BECAME THE FIRST PERSON TO REACH THE BOTTOM OF THIS PIT.

2,165

AT 2,165 FT (660 M), XIAOZHAI TIANKENG IN CHINA IS THE DEEPEST SINKHOLE IN THE WORLD.

SALT OF
THE EARTH

This eerie and endless **expanse of nothingness** is the **world's largest salt flat**—a dry lake bed with a perfectly flat salt crust. High on a Bolivian plateau, **Salar de Uyuni** gets covered in water when it rains, turning the surface into a **magnificent mirror**.

Stretching across 4,085 sq miles (10,582 sq km), the salt flat can be crossed on foot or by car because it is either dry or flooded by only a couple of inches of water.

SALTY STAY

Salt is so plentiful that a hotel has been built from salt in the Salar. Called Palacio de Sal ("Palace of Salt"), it dissolves in water, so must be repaired each time it rains.

THE SALT FORMS EYE-CATCHING **HEXAGON** SHAPES ON THE SURFACE.

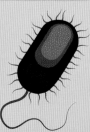

THE SALT FLATS ARE HOME TO A VARIETY OF **MICROSCOPIC LIFE**, INCLUDING BACTERIA.

FAST FACTS

The Salar has a bed of salt because during the rainy season, the water has nowhere to go. It evaporates, leaving behind any minerals it was carrying as salts.

Sea water
Water in the open ocean is about 3.5% salt.

3.5% salt

Salar de Uyuni
As the Salar dries up, its water becomes eight times saltier than the sea.

28% salt

Dead Sea
Some salt lakes, such as the Dead Sea, are even saltier than the Salar.

34% salt

A thin covering of water lies over a crust of salt up to 33 ft (10 m) thick.

Highlands within the Salar become islands when the lake bed floods. The islands are never drenched, so they have no salt crust. Plants such as cacti can survive on the islands' slopes.

Beneath the salt is one of the largest deposits of lithium, which is used in rechargeable batteries.

The dry lake bed that forms Salar de Uyuni was once part of a much larger prehistoric salt lake. Occasional rainfall covers the salt briefly in water, which dissolves the surface. As the water evaporates, the salt recrystallizes in a perfectly flat plain.

ABOUT 24,000 VISITORS TREK ACROSS THESE FLATS EVERY YEAR.

A LOCAL **FACTORY** PROCESSES THE SALT FROM THE SALAR DE UYUNI.

A TIME AND
A PLACE

Some places serve as reminders of the **past**. These **eerie sites** bear the scars of moments that **changed the landscape** forever.

Beach bomb
At the turn of the 20th century, the Mexican government bombed the uninhabited Marieta Islands for target practice. One bomb blasted out Hidden Beach, a picture-postcard paradise beach tucked underneath the shore.

THE ANCIENT CITY OF BAIAE, ITALY, SANK INTO THE OCEAN AFTER AN EARTHQUAKE, LEAVING MANY SCULPTURES ON THE OCEAN FLOOR.

A METEORITE STRIKE ABOUT 50,000 YEARS AGO CREATED THE BARRINGER CRATER IN ARIZONA.

Religious ruins
All that is left of the Mexican village of San Juan Parangaricutiro is the church. In 1943, the Parícutin volcano started smoking and eventually erupted, burying all the buildings except the church under rock and ash.

Unforgettable forts
In World War II, defensive forts were constructed off the UK's Kent coastline to protect the Thames estuary. The Maunsell Sea Forts are now open to the public, with seasonal boat tours to visit the isolated towers.

THE ANCIENT **ROMAN CITIES** OF POMPEII AND HERCULANEUM WERE BURIED BY THE ERUPTION OF MOUNT VESUVIUS.

IN 1956, A **SECRET BUNKER** WAS BUILT 213 FT (65 M) BELOW MOSCOW, RUSSIA, TO WITHSTAND A NUCLEAR ATTACK.

LAKE
SPOTTING

Canada's Okanagan Valley is home to a lake **like no other**. Its dazzling dots are caused by **high levels of minerals**. For centuries, **Spotted Lake** has been a **sacred site** for the First Nations (Canadian Indigenous peoples), who harnessed the **healing properties** of its mix of minerals.

WATER THERAPY

First Nations people used the lake's mud and water to treat aches, pains, and other medical problems. Legend has it that two warring tribes signed a truce so both groups could treat their injured warriors with the waters. In 2001, the Okanagan First Nations bought the site in order to protect it from development.

The lake's spots range from green and blue to white and yellow depending on the mixture of minerals they contain.

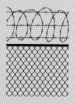

TOURISTS ARE ALLOWED TO VIEW THE LAKE ONLY FROM BEHIND A FENCE THAT PROTECTS THIS SITE.

SPOTTED LAKE IS SURROUNDED BY CAIRNS—ROCKY MOUNDS USED TO MARK GRAVES.

FAST FACTS

British Columbia, Canada

Washington, US

Wyoming, US

Arizona, US | New Mexico, US

Epsom, UK
Stassfurt, Germany
Mount Vesuvius, Italy
Hérault, France

South Africa

This map shows the main places where magnesium sulfate occurs naturally.

Magnesium sulfate is commonly known as Epsom salts, named after the town in Surrey, UK, where the mineral also occurs naturally. It has a range of medical uses, from treating boils to relieving constipation. Many athletes bathe in Epsom salts to soothe sore muscles and speed up recovery times.

y the city of Osoyoos in British Columbia lies ootted Lake. Its waters contain an unusually high ncentration of minerals, especially magnesium ilfate, calcium, and sodium sulfates, along with wer levels of at least 10 other minerals. In ummer, the water evaporates, leaving more than 00 individual pools in an array of different colors.

During
World War I,
the lake's
minerals were
used in Canadian
ammunition
factories.

Magnesium sulfate crystallizes in summer to form pathways around the lake's spots.

THE OKANAGAN FIRST NATIONS PURCHASED THIS SACRED SITE FOR $720,000.

SCIENTISTS HAVE STUDIED THIS LAKE TO UNDERSTAND THE GEOLOGICAL PROCESSES OF THE PLANET MARS.

MYSTERIOUS
WELLS

The **cenotes** ("sacred wells") of Mexico are **secret pools** with beautiful clear waters. These developed naturally around the Yucatán Peninsula when **cavern roofs collapsed**. The ancient Maya believed cenotes were entrances to the **mysterious underworld** of the gods.

ALL THAT REMAINS

Underwater archaeologists exploring Mexico's cenotes have found human skulls and bones, suggesting that the Maya carried out human sacrifices to honor their gods. The discoveries have scared villagers living near the cenotes today, who steer clear of these pools.

The Yucatán Peninsula is known for its porous limestone. Over time heavy rainfall caused the rock to give way in places, revealing spectacular groundwater pools underneath. The Maya set up homes nearby, making use of the pristine water supply. They thought the gods communicated at cenotes, so religious ceremonies were also performed there.

CENOTES ARE TEEMING WITH LIFE, INCLUDING FISH, CRABS, TURTLES, MANATEES, AND CROCODILES.

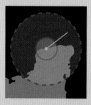

A RING OF CENOTES SURROUNDS THE **CHICXULUB CRATER**, WHICH WAS FORMED BY A METEORITE 66 MYA.

FAST FACTS

1,112 ft (339 m)   1,083 ft (330 m)

The deepest water-filled cenote in the world is also in Mexico. El Zacatón is 1,112 ft (339 m) deep— deeper than France's Eiffel Tower is high.

Tree roots dangle through the surface opening into the clear water of the cenote.

There are tens of thousands of beautiful cenotes in the Yucatán Peninsula.

SOME CENOTES LINK WITH EXTENSIVE CAVE SYSTEMS WHERE DIVERS HAVE FOUND EVIDENCE OF MINING BY EARLY HUMANS.

MAYA TREASURES OF GOLD AND JADE HAVE BEEN FOUND AT A SACRED CENOTE NEAR THE ANCIENT CITY OF CHICHÉN ITZÁ.

FAIRY
CHIMNEYS

These **magical stone structures** transform the Turkish terrain of Cappadocia into a fairy kingdom. Carved by the **forces of nature**, countless **ancient rock formations** tower over the surrounding valleys and villages.

The body of each chimney is made up of layers of limestone and volcanic ash.

Fairy chimneys **are named for their seemingly magical shapes**.

THE CAPPADOCIANS USED SIMPLE TOOLS TO CARVE THEIR HOMES.

MORE THAN 200 ANCIENT UNDERGROUND CITIES HAVE BEEN FOUND IN THIS REGION.

Fairy chimneys have explosive origins. Millions of years ago, volcanic activity resulted in layers of soft sedimentary rock, topped by a hard layer of basalt. At the mercy of wind and rain, the soft rock eroded gradually, transforming the landscape into distinctive shapes, including cones, columns, and mushrooms. Local people turned the chimneys into houses, churches, and monasteries.

FAIRY-TALE HOTELS

Some of the larger fairy chimneys have been hollowed out and sculpted into unique hotels. With cavelike rooms offering views of the colossal chimneys, visitors can enjoy the most authentic experience of Cappadocia.

The capped chimneys have a tough head of basalt, which protects the soft rock below.

FAST FACTS

Rivers of rainwater eroded the soft rock.

Several million years ago, volcanoes covered the area with volcanic ash, which was compressed into soft sedimentary rock. Rainwater and wind eroded this rock, leaving behind chimneylike formations protected by hard basalt caps. If a fairy chimney loses its basalt cap, it will eventually disappear completely.

SOME FAIRY CHIMNEYS WERE USED TO HOUSE PIGEONS—THEIR DROPPINGS WERE USED AS FERTILIZER.

HOT AIR BALLOON FLIGHTS OFFER VISITORS THE BEST VIEWS OF THIS FANTASTICAL LANDSCAPE.

RAINBOW
ROCKS

There's no need to roll out the red carpet at **Danxia** in **China's Gansu Province**. The jaw-dropping rocky landscape is **naturally red** from a buildup of sandstone over many millions of years, while the **rainbow effect** comes from **colorful mineral deposits**.

LIFE ON MARS

Another red world is Mars. It is called the "Red Planet" because of the dusty surface layer of orange-red iron oxide. Alien life-forms may have lived on Mars three billion years ago when it was warmer and had flowing water.

154 THESE COLORFUL ROCKS COVER AN AREA OF MORE THAN **154 SQ MILES** (400 SQ KM).

FOSSILS OF INSECTS, PLANTS, AND ANIMALS HAVE BEEN FOUND HERE.

The name **Danxia** means "rosy clouds" in Chinese.

Danxia's **crumpled landscape** comes from movement in Earth's crust, combined with wind and rain carving out ravines and pillars in the soft rock.

Danxia's rock formations have eroded naturally by wind and rain. This has created today's steep cliffs, solitary peaks, and textured layers. Danxia is the generic term for red sandstone landforms, but kaleidoscopic streaks of yellow, green, and blue from various mineral deposits add to the palette.

FAST FACTS

Over millions of years, sandstone and mineral deposits were compressed into multicolored layers of rock. Movement of the giant plates that form Earth's crust pushed, cut, and folded the layers.

Rain and wind gradually erode the surface, revealing more colored layers.

Bands of sandstone colored by different minerals are laid down.

Plate pushes in

Plate pushes in

The layers fold up as the plates push together.

A VIEWING **PLATFORM** NAMED "COLORFUL SEA OF CLOUDS" HAS A HILL POINT, ACCESSIBLE BY CLIMBING 666 STEPS.

A SANDSTONE STRUCTURE THAT LOOKS LIKE A ROCK **FORTRESS** LIES CLOSE BY.

ON THE
ROCKS

Wind and water constantly **batter** the planet's rocky regions, sculpting **unusual formations** that must be seen to be believed.

Sandstone spirals
Antelope Canyon, located in Diné (Navajo) Nation, in Arizona, is named after the herds of antelope that once inhabited the area. These breathtaking rocks were carved by wind and rainwater flooding through the canyon and eroding the sandstone into smooth, spiral structures.

 IT TAKES UP TO **FOUR HOURS** TO WALK AROUND ULURU, THE WORLD'S LARGEST SINGLE ROCK, LOCATED IN AUSTRALIA.

 A WEATHERED ROCK IN US'S BRYCE CANYON IS NAMED **THOR'S HAMMER** FOR ITS RESEMBLANCE TO THE NORSE GOD'S WEAPON.

Hobgoblin's playground
Little Finland in Nevada, USA, is named for the fins adorning the desert's red sandstone. The area is also called the Hobgoblin's playground because of its fantastical formations.

easide seat
orway's Kannesteinen ock is the eye-popping esult of years of coastal rosion. With its sea view verlooking Vågsøy Island, his distinctive formation s called "the Kanne chair" y locals.

Wipeout wave
The surf's always up at Wave Rock near Hyden, Australia. Stretching 49 ft (15 m) high and reaching 360 ft (110 m) wide, the huge rock resembles a breaking wave and is a sacred spot for local First Nation Australians.

12

THE THREE IMPOSING **GRANITE PEAKS** OF CHILE'S PAINE MOUNTAIN RANGE FORMED ABOUT 12 MILLION YEARS AGO.

KJERAGBOLTEN IS A BOULDER WEDGED IN A NORWEGIAN MOUNTAIN CREVASSE.

GLORIOUS
GEYSER

Fly Geyser in Black Rock Desert is no ordinary geyser. While many form naturally, this geyser was created in 1964 when a well was drilled on Fly Ranch but then sealed. Eventually, **superheated water** burst through the surface cracks, and the repeated eruptions have left behind **mineral deposits**, forming this dazzling rainbow-colored geyser.

Each time Fly Geyser erupts, it releases minerals that have dissolved in the scalding water. These minerals solidify when the water cools, creating an ever-growing mound surrounded by terraced rock pools. Vibrant red and green streaks over the mound are the result of thermophilic (heat-loving) algae thriving in the steamy surroundings.

SPOUTS IN SPACE

Geysers are not only found on Earth. Saturn's moon Enceladus (above) hosts 101 geysers, while geysers of water vapor were seen spouting on Jupiter's moon Europa in 2013.

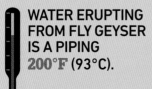

WATER ERUPTING FROM FLY GEYSER IS A PIPING **200°F** (93°C).

FLY GEYSER'S TERRACED POOLS ARE MADE OF **TRAVERTINE**, A TYPE OF ROCK USED TO MAKE BUILDINGS, INCLUDING ROME'S COLOSSEUM.

Water gushes **up** to 5 ft (1.5 m), filling nearby pools.

FAST FACTS

Geysers occur where underground water comes into contact with hot rocks. Under pressure, the water becomes superheated before reaching boiling point and making its way through cracks in the rock to erupt explosively through a surface vent.

The geyser erupts.

Groundwater soaks through layers of rock.

Water is heated further under pressure and rises to the surface.

Water is heated by contact with hot rocks.

Minerals in the water react with oxygen in the air to create an environment that allows colorful algae to grow.

The mound continues to grow, adding new layers to its height each year.

BLACK ROCK DESERT WAS ONCE A LAKE. TODAY, IT IS ONE OF THE FLATTEST PLACES ON EARTH.

295

YELLOWSTONE'S STEAMBOAT GEYSER, THE WORLD'S TALLEST ACTIVE GEYSER, HURLS WATER 295 FT (90 M) INTO THE AIR.

The Elephant Foot glacier is fed by smaller glacier ice on the edge of Greenland.

JUMBO
GLACIER

Eye-popping from the air, the **Elephant Foot Glacier** in Greenland is the exact shape of a giant jumbo's foot. Made from **compacted snow** over **hundreds of years**, this icy mass has **perfect proportions** and **stunning symmetry**.

Glaciers are masses of land-based ice, which develop at the poles or in areas of high altitude. There are several different types, but all are made from layers of snow and move slowly under their own immense weight. The Elephant Foot Glacier is a piedmont glacier. These glaciers are often formed when the ice from a steep valley glacier spills over an open plain.

PIEDMONT GLACIERS ARE FAN-SHAPED AND OFTEN ALMOST COMPLETELY SYMMETRICAL.

3 miles

THE TERMINUS (THE END OF THE GLACIER) IS ABOUT 3 MILES (5.4 KM) WIDE.

The mountains on either side of the glacier stand more than 3,280 ft (1,000 m) high, which helps convey the scale of this icy expanse.

FAST FACTS

Ground snow

Snowflakes

Granular ice

Firn

Glacier ice

In cold regions, snow does not melt but piles up in layers. The weight squeezes the snow beneath, forming grains of ice that gradually pack together until they become firn—a middle stage between snow and glacier ice. In a process that can take centuries, the air is squeezed out and the firn turns to dense glacier ice (see p.33).

SILVER-TONGUED GLACIER

The Erebus Ice Tongue in Antarctica is a tongue-like projection extending from the Erebus glacier. Stretching for 7 miles (11 km), parts of the icy tongue have been known to splinter off into the sea, where they become icebergs.

MOST GLACIERS FLOW SO SLOWLY THAT IT IS HARD TO DETECT ANY MOVEMENT.

MALASPINA IN ALASKA IS THE WORLD'S LARGEST PIEDMONT GLACIER, COVERING 1,500 SQ MILES (3,890 SQ KM).

On the hottest days, temperatures in the Danakil Depression soar to more than 122°F (50°C).

Sulfur and mineral salt give Danakil its striking colors.

EXPLOSIVE
HEAT

Few people can stand the **heat** of the **Danakil Depression** in Ethiopia. Active **volcanoes** sizzle inside this desert basin, and sulfur springs emit **choking gases**. No wonder some have called it the **cruelest place** on Earth.

LYING 410 FT (125 M) BELOW SEA LEVEL, THE DANAKIL DEPRESSION IS THE LOWEST POINT IN AFRICA.

WITH A YEAR-ROUND AVERAGE TEMPERATURE OF 93.2°F (34°C), THE DANAKIL DEPRESSION IS THE HOTTEST INHABITED PLACE ON EARTH.

FAST FACTS

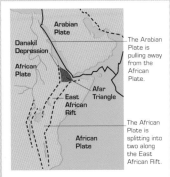

The Arabian Plate is pulling away from the African Plate.

The African Plate is splitting into two along the East African Rift.

The Afar Triangle is a vast low area created where Earth's tectonic plates are pulling apart. The huge forces in play, as Earth's crust is stretched and thinned, cause earthquakes and volcanic eruptions along the plate boundaries. The Danakil Depression, in the north of the triangle, owes its sulfur lakes and active volcanoes to these tectonic forces.

As well as fierce volcanoes and sulphur springs, the Danakil Depression in the Afar Triangle is home to acid lakes and occasional earthquakes. It has little to no rainfall and searing temperatures day and night. For centuries local merchants have collected salt from the region's salt flats, and today the most intrepid tourists brave the dangers to marvel at the otherworldly landscape.

EARLIEST ANCESTORS

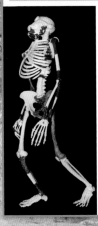

Fossilized remains of our earliest ancestors have been found in the Afar Triangle, not far from the Danakil Depression. In 1974 a team working here found the bones of an early hominid. Dubbed "Lucy" (reconstruction pictured), she is thought to have lived a mind-boggling 3.2 million years ago.

THE AIR SMELLS OF ROTTEN EGGS DUE TO THE VOLCANIC GASES AND SULFUR SPRINGS.

MOST OF ETHIOPIA'S SALT SUPPLY COMES FROM THE SALT MINED AT DANAKIL.

It **rains almost** every day **of the** year on **Mount Roraima**.

Mount Roraima means "big blue-green" in Pemón, a reference to its stunning lush vegetation and waterfalls.

ISLAND
IN THE SKY

Imagine a paradise island floating above the clouds and **two billion years** in the making. Welcome to **Mount Roraima** in South America, one of the world's **oldest mountain formations**, with panoramic views across the borders of **Venezuela**, **Brazil**, and **Guyana**.

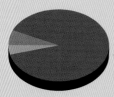

ABOUT 85% OF RORAIMA LIES IN VENEZUELA, WITH 10% IN GUYANA AND 5% IN BRAZIL.

MOUNT RORAIMA HOUSES THE WORLD'S LONGEST QUARTZ CAVE SYSTEM.

The flat summit covers 12 sq miles (31 sq km).

FAST FACTS

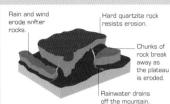

Rain and wind erode softer rocks.

Hard quartzite rock resists erosion.

Chunks of rock break away as the plateau is eroded.

Rainwater drains off the mountain.

Mount Roraima is what is known as a tabletop mountain because of its flat top. The flat summit was originally part of a huge sandstone plateau, which fragmented and eroded over millions of years, leaving the mountain towering over the surrounding lowlands.

This unusual mountain inspired Sir Arthur Conan Doyle's book about dinosaurs and humans, *The Lost World*.

TUMBLING TOADS

Mount Roraima is home to a diverse array of animals and plants. The strangest species living here are black pebble toads, said to predate the dinosaurs. Found in 1895, these tiny toads have limited mobility. Unable to swim or hop, they roll themselves into balls and bounce off rocks to escape attackers.

Mount Roraima is the highest peak in the dramatic Pakaraima Mountains. Indigenous peoples of America believe their gods inhabit these lush mountains, so they call the peaks *tepuis*, which translates in local Pemón as "houses of the gods."

SOME OF THE HIGHEST WATERFALLS ON EARTH DROP FROM THIS MOUNTAIN'S STEEP CLIFF FACES.

THE PITCHER PLANT *HELIAMPHORA*, WHICH TRAPS INSECTS FOR FOOD, WAS FIRST DISCOVERED ON MOUNT RORAIMA.

RAINBOW
SPRING

One of the world's largest hot springs, **Grand Prismatic Spring** is located in the US's Yellowstone National Park. Explorers gave the spring its name in 1871 after witnessing its incredible **prism of colors**. Measuring 370 ft (113 m) wide and 121 ft (37 m) deep, it releases 560 gallons (2,120 liters) of water a minute.

FIRES OF HELL

The city of Beppu in Japan is home to eight fiery natural springs, known as *jigoku* ("hells"). The Blood Pond Hot Spring is the most famous because of its steaming red waters. This color comes from high levels of iron in the area.

YELLOWSTONE NATIONAL PARK IS HOME TO 500 GEYSERS—MORE THAN HALF OF THE WORLD'S TOTAL.

ABOUT 4,500 BISON USE YELLOWSTONE'S HOT SPRINGS TO KEEP WARM DURING THE WINTER MONTHS.

The water at the center of the spring can reach a searing 189°F (87°C).

The kaleidoscope effect is caused by colorful bacteria, which thrive in these superhot springs. In the blue center is near-boiling water. This gradually cools across the spring's surface, and as the temperature changes, different types of bacteria are able to survive. The bacteria living in different parts of the spring are brightly colored, giving Grand Prismatic its characteristic rainbow rings.

The blue area at the spring's center is too hot to sustain most life-forms.

FAST FACTS

The Grand Prismatic Spring is named for its colors, which match the spectrum of white light through a prism. When white light passes through a triangular block of glass (a prism), it splits into wavelengths of different colors.

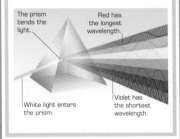

The prism bends the light.

Red has the longest wavelength.

White light enters the prism.

Violet has the shortest wavelength.

VISITORS BATHE IN THE MINERAL-RICH BEPPU HOT SPRINGS TO SOOTHE THEIR ACHES AND PAINS.

NEW ZEALAND'S WAIMANGU CAULDRON, THE WORLD'S BIGGEST HOT SPRING, HAS A CONSTANT TEMPERATURE OF 122–140°F (50–60°C).

DEEP
FREEZE

Meaning **"glacier of rivers,"** Iceland's
Vatnajökull is the **largest glacier**
in Europe. Underneath the ice
is a **frozen world** called the Crystal
Caves, a **hidden labyrinth** of
blue chambers and tunnels
that change with the seasons.

The location of the ice
caves tends to shift every
year as water melts and
freezes again.

ADVANCING ICE

Stretching for 19 miles (30 km),
Perito Moreno in Argentina
is an unusual glacier because
it is advancing, rather than
shrinking. Heavy chunks of ice
break off regularly, dropping
into the shimmering waters
of Lake Argentino.

HVANNADALSHNÚKUR,
ICELAND'S **HIGHEST
MOUNTAIN** AT 7,218 FT
(2,200 M), LIES
BENEATH
VATNAJÖKULL.

THE VAST
GLACIER
COVERS **8%**
OF ICELAND'S
SURFACE AREA.

In the summer sunshine the surface of Vatnajökull's thick glacial ice melts, and the resulting water flows into holes and cracks on the surface. Underneath the glacier, rivers of this meltwater cut through the ancient glacier ice, leaving behind magnificent glacial caves. Each year the caves appear in different places—local guides scout their location and take tourists to those that are safe to visit.

FAST FACTS

Seven colors make up the white light that we see.

Only the blue light is scattered.

Dense glacier ice absorbs most of the colors.

Why is the ice blue?
Thick, dense glacier ice doesn't contain air bubbles, which would scatter lots of light and make the ice appear white. Rather, the ice absorbs most of the colors that make up white light and scatters only the blue—which is what you see.

The **ice** comprising the **Vatnajökull glacier is about 1,000 years old**.

THE CRYSTAL CAVES CAN BE **EXPLORED** DURING THE WINTER MONTHS.

SCIENTISTS ESTIMATE THAT THE GLACIER HAS BEEN **SHRINKING** BY 3 FT (1 M) EVERY YEAR AND WILL EVENTUALLY DISAPPEAR.

COOL
CAVES

Hidden away deep inside **Earth's crust** is a magical **subterranean world** of caverns, such as these stunning examples.

Psychedelic salt mine
A former salt mine in Yekaterinburg, Russia, is now one of the world's most colorful caves. Some 650 ft (200 m) underground, its patterned rainbow walls are caused by the mineral carnallite swirling in layers through the rock.

THE **WINDING TUNNELS** OF YEKATERINBURG'S SALT MINE EXTEND FOR MORE THAN 4 MILES (6 KM).

THE **SALT** IN THIS RUSSIAN MINE FORMED FROM EVAPORATING SEAWATER ABOUT 280 MILLION YEARS AGO.

Crystal caves

Only discovered in 2000, the Cave of Crystals in Mexico is part of a mine near the town of Naica and is home to the largest crystals in the world. Some of the giant selenite crystals it contains have grown to more than 33 ft (10 m) in length.

Marble marvels

Crashing waves have eroded and sculpted Patagonia's Marble Caves. One of the caves is called the Marble Cathedral, after its distinctive sweeping arches. Eye-catching reflections of the shimmering blue water dance across white marble ceilings.

950

MEXICO'S **CAVE OF CRYSTALS** LIES 950 FT (290 M) BELOW THE GROUND.

THE MARBLE CATHEDRAL IS **ACCESSIBLE** ONLY BY BOAT OR KAYAK.

STONE
FOREST

Like an enchanted forest that's been turned to stone, **Grand Tsingy** in Madagascar is a sombre scene of **spiky, treelike rocks**. The world's largest stone forest was carved by **tropical rain** in a process that lasted millions of years.

Tsingy de Bemaraha **covers a vast 230 sq miles (600 sq km).**

The canyon walls are up to 328 ft (100 m) tall.

The razor-sharp, vertical stones of Grand Tsingy challenge even the most experienced rock climbers.

EXTREME LIVING

A surprising number of species call Tsingy de Bemaraha National Park their home. More than 100 types of birds, at least 30 types of reptiles, and 11 types of lemurs, including the Von der Decken's sifaka (above), live here. Many are found nowhere else in the world.

THE ROCKS ARE **SHARP ENOUGH** TO CUT THROUGH TOUGH HIKING BOOTS.

LEMURS CAN BE SPOTTED JUMPING FROM ONE ROCKY PEAK TO ANOTHER.

Meaning **"where one cannot walk,"** Grand Tsingy is an isolated wilderness in Madagascar's Tsingy de Bemaraha National Park. Its limestone rock has been eroded into a gridlike pattern of dead straight canyons called grikes, topped with dangerously craggy spears. Though the entire area appears gray rather than green, plant life flourishes between the peaks.

FAST FACTS

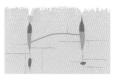

Groundwater flowing along fracture lines in the rock cut caves in the limestone of Grand Tsingy, while monsoon rains eroded the surface.

Over millions of years, the water continued to erode the caves, causing them to expand and merge into deep, narrow underground caverns.

The cave ceilings then collapsed, exposing the network of towering canyons we see today, topped with sharp peaks carved by surface erosion.

ABOUT **85%** OF THE SPECIES FOUND IN THE NATIONAL PARK ARE UNIQUE TO MADAGASCAR.

WOBBLY **ROPE BRIDGES** ARE THE ONLY WAY TO CROSS THE DEEP GORGES.

RED
ALERT!

Tanzania's Lake Natron has a **killer reputation**. Said to **turn local wildlife to stone**, its bright red waters certainly seem to **signal danger**. But in fact, the concentration of harmful chemicals in this **alkaline lake** supports a rich ecosystem.

THRIVING FLAMINGOS

Despite the dangers, about 2.5 million lesser flamingos nest on Lake Natron, making it one of the largest breeding grounds for this African species. They build their nests on small islands that form in the lake during the dry season and feed on the plentiful algae inhabiting the waters.

Alkali salt deposits have formed a crisscross pattern on the lake.

The blood-red color is caused by microorganisms that thrive in the salty waters.

FLAMINGOS HAVE TOUGH SKIN THAT PROTECTS THEM FROM GETTING BURNED BY THE CAUSTIC WATER.

AS MANY AS 300,000 FLAMINGO CHICKS GATHER AROUND THE SHALLOW WATERS OF THE LAKE UNTIL THEY ARE READY TO FLY.

Algae thrive in the hot springs on the lake's shores, providing food for alkaline tilapia, a fish adapted to live in this extreme environment.

The **water** of Lake Natron reaches **scalding temperatures** of more than **104°F (40°C).**

Fed by hot springs, Lake Natron's waters are rich in minerals. These chemicals are so concentrated that the lake is highly alkaline—with a pH level of 10, it is the most caustic body of water in the world (capable of burning the eyes and skin of creatures that are not adapted to it). The lake takes its name from natron (hydrated sodium carbonate), which is left as a salt deposit when lake water evaporates.

This lake contains minerals that come from hot springs, the lake's volcanic bedrock, and the ash from a nearby volcano.

FAST FACTS

Just 12 miles (20 km) away from Lake Natron lies Ol Doinyo Lengai, the only active volcano in the world that erupts "cold" lava. Unlike normal, silicate-rich lava, the molten rock it spews forth contains calcium, carbon dioxide, and sodium. It erupts at about 932°F (500°C)—very hot, but half of the temperature of normal lava—and emerges black, rather than red, cooling to stark white.

The volcano's summit looks snowcapped but, in fact, is covered in ash.

Ol Doinyo Lengai is 9,711 ft (2,960 m) high, with a classic cone shape.

35 THE LAKE IS ABOUT **35 MILES** (57 KM) LONG BUT ONLY 10 FT (3 M) DEEP.

NATRON WAS AN IMPORTANT INGREDIENT FOR THE **ANCIENT EGYPTIANS**— THEY USED IT DURING MUMMIFICATION AND FOR MAKING GLASS.

GIANT'S
CAUSEWAY

Hailed as the **eighth wonder of the world**, the Giant's Causeway on the north coast of Northern Ireland consists of a pathway of about **40,000** interlocking **basalt columns**. A **famous legend** explains its creation, but it really resulted from a **volcanic eruption**.

The **earliest account of** the Causeway's existence dates from **1693**.

MYSTERY MEN

Chalk outlines of giant human figures seen on the English landscape date back to the Iron Age. Locals living near the Long Man of Wilmington (above) in East Sussex and the Cerne Abbas Giant in Dorset traditionally associated them with luck and fertility.

ALTHOUGH MOST COLUMNS ARE SIX-SIDED, SOME ARE FOUR-, FIVE-, SEVEN-, AND EVEN EIGHT-SIDED.

SOME OF THE FORMATIONS HAVE NAMES, INCLUDING THE WISHING CHAIR AND THE GIANT'S BOOT.

FAST FACTS

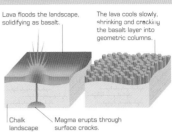

Lava floods the landscape, solidifying as basalt.

The lava cools slowly, shrinking and cracking the basalt layer into geometric columns.

Chalk landscape

Magma erupts through surface cracks.

Giant's Causeway was created by intense volcanic activity 50–60 million years ago. Magma burst through cracks in Earth's surface, flooding the landscape with layers of lava. Cracks formed as the lava cooled, resulting in thousands of regular columns of basalt.

The Wishing Chair is a natural throne formed amidst the columns, and in the past, only women were allowed to sit on it.

Legend goes that giant Finn McCool created a causeway from Ireland to Scotland to challenge rival Scottish giant Benandonner. When enormous Benandonner appeared, McCool's wife Oonagh hatched a cunning plan. McCool pretended to be a big baby, leaving his rival terrified of how huge the father must be! Benandonner raced home along the causeway to Scotland.

THE CAUSEWAY IS A SAFE HAVEN FOR NESTING COLONIES OF BIRDS, SUCH AS CORMORANTS.

MANY SHIPWRECKS HAVE BEEN FOUND NEAR THE CAUSEWAY— SOME WITH PRICELESS TREASURE.

Human wonders

There is no limit to imagination. People have always made their mark on the world, from ancient innovations and contemporary constructions to death-defying endeavors and thrill-seeking stunts. All around the planet, different cultures enrich their environments, sometimes in the most unexpected ways.

The world's largest ice festival has been held annually at Harbin in northeastern China since 1985. Packed with sculptures, the "Ice City" is best seen at night when its ice castles and lanterns are illuminated.

FAST FACTS

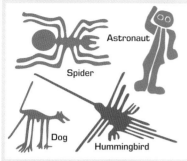

Astronaut

Spider

Dog

Hummingbird

The mysterious lines are found on a coastal plain between two river valleys. There are hundreds of individual designs, and many more shapes and straight lines. They were created over several centuries, with some newer geoglyphs overlapping or obscuring older ones. In 2014 previously unknown geoglyphs were uncovered by a sandstorm.

Crafted between 500 BCE and 500 CE, the Nazca lines include images of animals, birds, and humanlike figures. The reason for their construction remains uncertain. Some historians believe the lines were art created for the gods to enjoy, while others speculate that they were maps of underground water sources or an early form of calendar.

The geoglyphs cover a vast area of about **174 sq miles (450 sq km).**

The huge lines were created by removing the dark top layer of gravel to reveal the lighter-colored earth underneath.

NAZCA WORSHIP

The Nazca people believed that worshipping the gods was key to survival. Their expertly crafted pottery features depictions of their gods, as well as nature spirits and mythical creatures. The Nazca had no writing system, so painting pots would have been one means of communicating their beliefs.

MOST NAZCA LINES ARE ETCHED ACROSS THE LANDSCAPE—SOME ARE 30 MILES (48 KM) LONG.

THE PICTURES OF ANIMALS AND PEOPLE WERE DRAWN AS A CONTINUOUS LINE, POSSIBLY USING A WOODEN STAKE.

DESERT
DRAWINGS

Aircraft pilots flying over Peru's **Nazca Desert** in the 1930s were amazed to see huge drawings **scratched into the landscape**. These **geoglyphs** are called **Nazca lines**, after the ancient Nazcas who made them, and they are a fascinating tribute to a **lost people**.

The monkey has three toes on each foot, four fingers on one hand, and five on the other. Some historians think the number of digits may have had a hidden meaning.

This geoglyph represents a monkey and measures 180 ft (55 m) long.

ARTIFICIAL INTELLIGENCE HAS BEEN USED TO IDENTIFY 143 NEW NAZCA DESIGNS, INCLUDING A **HUMANLIKE FIGURE**.

WELL-PRESERVED **MUMMIES** OF ANCIENT NAZCA PEOPLE HAVE BEEN DISCOVERED IN PERU.

LIFE-SIZE
CLAY WARRIORS

A **chance discovery** of a hidden pit in Xi'an, China, led to an incredible find—nearly **8,000 life-size soldiers** sculpted **2,200 years ago**. Called the **Terracotta Army**, these clay figures were crafted to protect the tomb of China's **First Emperor**, Qin Shi Huang.

Statues were originally painted in bright colours.

EXTENSIVE EXCAVATIONS

Four pits were found, but the last was empty, suggesting the mausoleum was incomplete when the emperor died. Many warriors lay in pieces and were painstakingly restored. Scientists think they were preserved due to the consistent temperature from burial until excavation.

A HUGE TEAM OF MORE THAN 700,000 WORKERS **CRAFTED** THE TERRACOTTA ARMY.

661

THE HEAVIEST CLAY SOLDIERS **WEIGH** A WHOPPING 661 LB (300 KG) EACH.

FAST FACTS

One of the warriors' huge crossbows could fire an arrow the length of seven and a half soccer fields.

The warriors' weapons were real but never used in battle. Thousands of bronze spears, battleaxes, crossbows, and arrowheads have been uncovered in superb condition. One crossbow found was about 5 ft (1.5 m) long and was capable of firing an arrow up to 2,600 ft (792 m).

The **emperor's tomb** lies **0.93 miles (1.5 km) away** at **Mount Li.**

Every detail was considered—even shoe soles, where visible, had their own intricate pattern.

In 1974, Chinese farmers were digging a well when they uncovered the pit housing the Terracotta Army. Archaeologists later found the soldiers inside. Lined up according to rank, there are archers, charioteers, officers, generals, and horsemen. A production line approach was used to make each warrior, with every body part crafted separately before the figure was fully assembled at the end.

EACH SOLDIER'S **FACE** IS DETAILED AND DIFFERENT, SUGGESTING THEY WERE MODELED ON REAL PEOPLE.

BURIED WITH THE SOLDIERS WERE 130 CHARIOTS, 520 HORSES, AND 150 CAVALRY HORSES.

COLORFUL
ENDINGS

Funerals in the West African country of Ghana are **upbeat gatherings**. Innovative coffins **celebrate** the deceased's work or interests.

Flight of fancy
Two brothers created this wooden aircraft coffin for their grandmother, who had never been in a plane but dreamed of flying.

Snap happy
Many coffins reflect the deceased's career, such as this camera-shaped coffin for a photographer.

 COFFIN COLORS **SYMBOLIZE** EACH PERSON, FOR EXAMPLE, RED REPRESENTS A FIERY PERSONALITY.

 COFFINS ARE MADE WITH **HAND TOOLS** BEFORE BEING PAINTED BY HAND TOO.

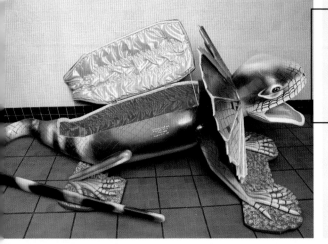

Coffin art
Examples of the handcrafted, ornately decorated caskets have been displayed all over the world. This lizard coffin was created for an exhibition in Melbourne, Australia.

Final fizz
No need to guess the deceased's drink of choice. Favorite foods can also be reflected in the shape of a coffin.

Luxury at a price
Fantasy coffins offer lavishly lined interiors—as this open leopard coffin shows—and cost more than $1,100 each. This is very expensive for many people, so usually only wealthy Ghanaians can afford them.

A COFFIN IN THE SHAPE OF A MERCEDES-BENZ IS POPULAR WITH WEALTHIER FAMILIES.

GHANAIAN COCOA FARMERS ARE OFTEN BURIED IN COFFINS SHAPED LIKE COCOA PODS.

THE SECRET
UNDERGROUND CITY

Turkey's ancient underground caves of **Cappadocia** were once **inhabited cities**. Steep, hollowed hillsides mask a **secret subterranean world**.

> Derinkuyu **is about 279 ft (85 m) deep**, carved out of volcanic rock.

Derinkuyu had **18 floors** and a network of random tunnels to deter would-be invaders.

1963 DERINKUYU LAY HIDDEN UNTIL 1963, WHEN IT WAS **DISCOVERED** DURING RENOVATIONS TO A BASEMENT.

THE UNDERGROUND CITIES WERE **CARVED** FROM THE LOCAL ROCK WITH SIMPLE TOOLS.

The deepest of Cappadocia's underground cities, Derinkuyu had sleeping quarters, communal rooms, bathrooms, cooking pits, wells, ventilation shafts, churches, and stables for animals. Historians believe this was the hiding place for early Christians trying to flee persecution from the Roman Empire.

FAST FACTS

One of about 200 cities, Derinkuyu had more than 600 entrances hidden in the courtyards of houses above ground. The city's inhabitants used heavy circular stone doors to block tunnels from the inside in the event of an attack.

The stone was rolled into the narrow passage and wedged from behind to block attackers.

DOWN UNDER

Sweltering summer temperatures made life difficult for locals in the Australian opal mining town of Coober Pedy, so, in 1915, they decided to retreat underground. Most of the town's 2,500 inhabitants still live underground in homes known as dugouts.

ABOUT 5 MILES (8 KM) OF TUNNELS LINKED DERINKUYU WITH THE NEIGHBORING SUBTERRANEAN CITY OF KAYMAKLI.

AT ITS PEAK, THE CITY OF DERINKUYU MAY HAVE HOUSED UP TO 20,000 PEOPLE.

MYSTERIOUS
MOAI

Standing head and shoulders above the volcanic lan
of **Rapa Nui** (also known as Easter Island) are moai-
huge human heads carved from rock more than **50
years** ago. Created by the **ancient Polynesians**, th
sculptures are still **sacre**
to today's islander:

FAMOUS FACES

Mount Rushmore, in
South Dakota is famous
for its cliff carvings of
four US presidents—
George Washington,
Thomas Jefferson,
Theodore Roosevelt,
and Abraham Lincoln.
From 1927 until their
completion in 1941,
about 400 people
worked on the faces.

**Rapa Nui is
1,200 miles
(1,900 km)
away from its
nearest island
neighbor.**

MANY MOAI
HEADS FEATURED
RED STONE
HATS KNOWN AS
PUKAO (TOPKNOTS).

15 AHU TONGARIKI IS THE
LARGEST CEREMONIAL
STRUCTURE WITH
15 STATUES STANDING
ALONG THE COASTLINE.

The average height of a moai is 13 ft (4 m) and the average weight is 14 tons.

The moai (statues) are testament to the extraordinary capabilities of the ancient Polynesians because they were difficult to construct and tough to transport around Rapa Nui. There are about 1,000 statues, all of them male. Most experts believe the moai were meant to honor the spirits of deceased ancestors, existing chiefs, or others special to the Polynesians, but nothing has been proven.

FAST FACTS

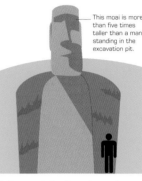

This moai is more than five times taller than a man standing in the excavation pit.

A large part of each moai is unseen because it is buried underground. The height of the tallest statue ever erected on Rapa Nui is about 33 ft (10 m).

The biggest statue, nicknamed El Gigante, was found in a quarry. This mega moai is 72 ft (22 m) tall and weighs about 176 tons— as much as a large blue whale.

WHITE **CORAL AND OBSIDIAN** WERE INSERTED INTO THE EYE SOCKETS DURING A CEREMONY TO AWAKEN THE MOAI.

ABOUT 400 OF THE MOAI ON RAPA NUI WERE **DISCOVERED** IN THE RANO RARAKU QUARRY.

DEEP
BREATH

The depths some people dive will **take your breath away**. From the earliest times, people have taken the plunge, but today **free diving** (diving without breathing equipment) is an **extreme sport** that pushes the human body to its **absolute limit**. Participants plumb the depths on just one **deep breath**.

FREE DIVING FOR FOOD

The Bajau people of Borneo are real water babies. Their houses stand on stilts in the sea, and they free dive in search of fish to eat. The best Bajau free divers can stay submerged on a single breath for up to five minutes, diving to the bottom of the reef, up to 230 ft (70 m) below.

As the depth increases, so does the amount of water pressing down on free diver Pierre Frolla from above. Free divers must learn to cope with the extreme conditions.

FREE DIVERS IN ANCIENT TIMES **SEARCHED FOR** FOOD, PEARLS, AND SPONGES ON THE OCEAN FLOOR.

SOME BAJAU DIVERS CAN **STAY UNDERWATER** FOR 13 MINUTES, REACHING DEPTHS OF UP TO 200 FT (60 M).

At a depth
of **328 ft (100 m)**,
water pressure
**compresses
human lungs**
to the size
of **fists**.

This **wreck** of
an aircraft is in
the Bahamas.

FAST FACTS

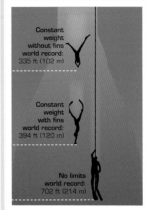

Constant
weight
without fins
world record:
335 ft (102 m)

Constant
weight
with fins
world record:
394 ft (120 m)

No limits
world record:
702 ft (214 m)

Competitive free diving
has different disciplines
depending on what
equipment the diver
uses. "No limits" free diving
involves using a weight
and cable to descend
very quickly. "Constant
weight" free divers
descend and ascend under
their own power. They
can use a weight to help
them descend but must
return to the surface
with the same weight.

**Holding their breath for minutes
at a time**, free divers plunge to
depths of more than 328 ft (100 m).
Divers train themselves for the
challenge mentally and physically,
but in some ways the human body
is hardwired to undertake this
amazing aquatic activity. When
submerged in cold water, the heart
rate slows to conserve oxygen. The
blood moves away from the arms
and legs to protect the vital organs.

CUVIER'S BEAKED WHALES ARE
RECORD-BREAKING MARINE MAMMALS,
DIVING UP TO 9,800 FT (3,000 M).

**EMPEROR
PENGUINS**
DIVE UP TO
1,854 FT (565 M)—
DEEPER THAN ANY
OTHER SEABIRD.

WET AND
WILD

Crossing the raging rapids of Asia's **Mekong River** on a precarious rope bridge is part of the daily routine for **local Lao fishermen**. However high the water, they must navigate the **dangerous currents** to secure a top spot and net a big catch.

At least **1,200 species** of fish inhabit the **Mekong River**.

SCHOOL'S OUT

The school run is a challenge in some parts of the world. These pupils must walk for two hours each day to attend their school in the mountains of Bijie, Guizhou Province, China. As well as passing through narrow tunnels in the rock, they must negotiate this treacherous cliff path, which is just 1.6 ft (0.5 m) wide.

ABOUT 300 MILLION PEOPLE LIVE BY THE MEKONG RIVER, A REGION INHABITED FOR 4,000 YEARS.

ABOUT ONE QUARTER OF THE WORLD'S FRESHWATER FISH COME FROM THE MEKONG RIVER.

With swirling rapids and crashing waterfalls, the Mekong River is unpredictable, experiencing huge fluctuations in flow throughout the year. But the river's wild waters contain a large variety of fish, making fishing the most common occupation for Mekong's riverside dwellers. This fisherman is risking a treacherous trip over a makeshift bridge to reach a prime fishing spot.

This precarious tightrope was built by a local fisherman using bits of rope and old cable.

The Chinese name for Mekong translates as "turbulent river," while the Thai and Lao name means "mother water." The Vietnamese call it "nine ragons" after the Mekong Delta's many tributaries.

FAST FACTS

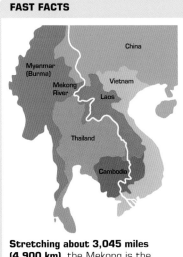

China

Myanmar (Burma)

Vietnam

Mekong River

Laos

Thailand

Cambodia

Stretching about 3,045 miles (4,900 km), the Mekong is the world's 12th longest river. It flows through China, Myanmar, Thailand, Laos, Cambodia, and Vietnam.

AN ENORMOUS FRESHWATER STINGRAY CAUGHT IN THE RIVER WEIGHED A RECORD-BREAKING 661 LB (300 KG).

THE MEKONG IS HOME TO THE IRRAWADDY DOLPHIN, ONE OF ONLY SIX RIVER DOLPHINS.

HONEY
HUNTERS

The **Gurung tribesmen** of Nepal make a living by collecting honeycomb from **gravity-defying** Himalayan cliffs. They put themselves in the **stickiest** of situations, dangling from rope ladders to access the sweet treat.

Blisters and bee stings are common complaints, but honey hunting can be fatal.

RISKY BUSINESS

Honey hunters in the Sundarbans forests of Bangladesh run the risk of tiger attacks. They light fires beside cliffs to smoke the bees out, but many hunters are injured or killed when the big cats come to investigate.

 50% OF BANGLADESH'S HONEY COMES FROM THE SUNDARBANS, THE LARGEST MANGROVE FOREST.

 MOST OF THE HONEY COLLECTED BY THE GURUNG TRIBESMEN IS SOLD, BUT SOME IS KEPT TO MAKE TEA.

Balancing precariously up to 90 m (300 ft) above the ground, honey hunters use thick smoke to sedate huge swarms of angry bees. This tradition has been going on for thousands of years.

Honey hunters use *tangos* – tools adapted from bamboo sticks – to cut the honey from the cliff face.

FAST FACTS

Measuring up to 1.2 in (3 cm) in length, the Himalayan giant honey bee (*Apis laboriosa*) is the largest honey bee in the world. It lives at high altitude and builds its large, precarious nests on the sides of vertical cliffs.

The Western honey bee is just 0.5 in (1.2 cm) long.

Himalayan giant honey bee

THE HIMALAYAN RED HONEY COLLECTED IN SPRING TIME IS PRIZED FOR ITS MEDICINAL BENEFITS.

AS WELL AS TIGERS, CROCODILES AND SNAKES PRESENT DANGERS IN THE SUNDARBANS.

SNOW
SCULPTURES

Since 1950, the world's biggest annual **celebration of snow** has caused flurries of excitement at **Sapporo** in Japan. More than **2.4 million visitors** descend on the city to wonder at the **snow sculptures** and toast the winner of the coolest competition around.

The amount of snow used at the festival is the equivalent of 6,500 five-ton trucks.

SNOWY SANCTUARY

The Hôtel de Glace in Quebec, Canada, is a dream destination for snow bunnies. The hotel is crafted almost entirely from snow and ice, offering visitors an ice chapel for wedding ceremonies, an ice slide, and an ice bar.

Fairy-tale castles and giant figures are among the sculptures on display.

400

THE SAPPORO SNOW FESTIVAL SHOWCASES ABOUT 400 EYE-CATCHING SNOW AND ICE **STATUES**.

THIS WINTER WONDERLAND OFFERS SKI JUMPING, **ICE SKATING**, SNOW SLIDING, AND SNOW RAFTING.

At the **Sapporo Snow Festival**, held every February, teams from around the world compete to develop the most imaginative and incredible snow sculptures. What began on a small scale, with school students displaying amateur efforts at the city's Odori Park, has grown to become one of the largest global events in the winter calendar, featuring hundreds of sculptures.

The **largest snow sculptures** can reach 50 ft (15 m) tall and 80 ft (24 m) wide.

FAST FACTS

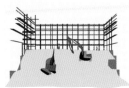

Sculpting starts with trucks transporting snow to the site, where bulldozers pack it into a firm base.

A frame is packed with more snow to form a solid block. The wooden boards are removed and carving begins.

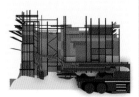

The frame is removed for the final details. Teams have just 20 hours from start to finish to create their art.

A SCARF-WEARING SNOWMAN IS THE OFFICIAL **MASCOT** FOR THIS FREEZING FESTIVAL.

1972

IN 1972, SAPPORO HOSTED THE WINTER **OLYMPIC GAMES**, HIGHLIGHTING THE CITY'S LONG-RUNNING SNOW FESTIVAL.

PLANE SPOTTER'S
PARADISE

The **jet blast** from the aircraft could **knock over or even kill a person** in its path.

One of the Caribbean's busiest airports, Princess Juliana International on Saint Martin island has unintentionally become a tourist attraction due to its low-flying aircraft. Saint Martin is the smallest island to be split between two nations. Holland and France share the idyllic isle, with Maho Beach on the Dutch side.

A ROUND ON THE RUNWAY

Kantarat's 18-hole golf course is tightly sandwiched between two runways of Thailand's Don Mueang Airport. Traffic lights help golf carts to cruise between holes safely.

COLORFUL **SURFBOARDS** ON MAHO BEACH DISPLAY THE FLIGHT TIMES FOR AIRCRAFT ARRIVALS.

AT LEAST **58,000** AIRCRAFT TAKE OFF OR LAND AT PRINCESS JULIANA AIRPORT EVERY YEAR.

Maho Beach is no peaceful paradise. Its blue skies are overshadowed by **low-flying jets**, while the crashing Caribbean surf is drowned out by **roaring engines**. With the runway just yards from the sand, thrill seekers and plane spotters can experience **extreme encounters** with aircraft every single day.

Sunbathers face powerful winds of 150 mph (240 km/h) every time an aircraft comes in to land.

FAST FACTS

With Princess Juliana's short runway of 7,152 ft (2,180 m), aircraft must fly at low altitude to land safely. As they make their descent, they pass just 30–60 ft (9–18 m) above the beach.

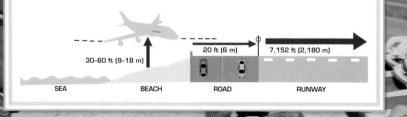

30–60 ft (9–18 m)   20 ft (6 m)   7,152 ft (2,180 m)

SEA   BEACH   ROAD   RUNWAY

COMMUNICATIONS BETWEEN INCOMING PILOTS AND THE AIR TRAFFIC CONTROL TOWER ARE BROADCAST OVER LOUD SPEAKERS.

PRINCESS JULIANA AIRPORT WELCOMES ABOUT TWO MILLION PASSENGERS EVERY YEAR.

FAST FACTS

One of the world's highest bungee jumps is from the Macau Tower in China. Sending thrill seekers spiraling down from a 764 ft (233 m) platform on the tower's outer rim, there is a six-second free fall before the elastic bounces back. The top height for a Naghol diving tower is 130 ft (40 m)—you'd have to stack about six end to end to match the Macau bungee.

Macau Tower

Naghol diving towers

BUNGEE JUMPING USES ELASTICIZED RUBBER CORDS THAT EXTEND UP TO **THREE TIMES** THEIR LENGTH.

NAGHOL DIVING IS ONLY PERMITTED FOR **2 MONTHS**, BETWEEN APRIL AND JUNE, AFTER THE WET SEASON.

LEAP OF
FAITH

Land diving takes place after the wet season—the vines have to be waterlogged to maximize their elasticity and strength.

Before bungee jumping, there was a scarier sport. A **daredevil diving ritual** called Naghol has been a tradition for centuries on **Pentecost Island**, part of the country of Vanuatu in the South Pacific. Local men risk life and limb to throw themselves from **dizzy heights** with only a **jungle vine** around their ankles.

Land diving is a rite of passage for the island's young men.

Land diving was first performed from treetops, but now fragile towers have been constructed. Before the jump, men and women chant and dance until one man climbs the tower, where vines are attached to his ankles. The diver jumps headfirst, dropping to the ground rapidly. Locals believe that the braver the divers are, the more bountiful the yam harvest will be.

LUCKY ESCAPE

The land diving ritual stems from a legend of an unhappy marriage, in which a woman was running through the jungle desperate to escape her husband. She climbed a tree with him hot on her heels, tied a vine to her ankle, and jumped. She landed safely, but her husband did not secure himself and did not survive the jump.

ISLANDERS TURN OVER THE SOIL TO CREATE A SOFTER LANDING FOR NAGHOL DIVERS.

IN 2006, THE VANUATU CULTURAL CENTRE BANNED ANY FILMING OF NAGHOL DIVING.

The **Street View Trekker** camera can also be worn **as a backpack**.

Raffia and her guide trekked the desert from sunrise to capture the best lighting for their shots.

TIMING IS EVERYTHING

When the Street View car cameras have been in the right place at the right time, they have caught rainbows (above), lightning strikes, and butterflies landing on their lenses. But when the timing goes wrong, birds narrowly miss crashing into cameras, while their poop seriously spoils the view!

SHEEP MOUNTED WITH GOOGLE CAMERAS HAVE MAPPED THE FAROE ISLANDS.

IN 2017, STREET VIEW DEVICES WERE PLACED ON THE **INTERNATIONAL SPACE STATION**.

FAST FACTS

Street View covers more than 10 million miles (16 million km) of road, across more than 80 countries, and continues to add more images. In addition to cities and towns, the project has captured panoramas of iconic sites such as the pyramids of Giza and Everest Base Camp.

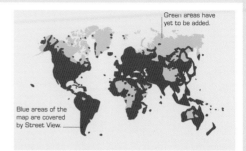

Green areas have yet to be added.

Blue areas of the map are covered by Street View.

Google Maps has been providing Google Street View online since 2007. The panoramic views it provides are made of still photographs, often captured by a car-mounted camera. But the Liwa Desert in the United Arab Emirates is not the average street view. These sprawling dunes needed a unique photographer, and an animal already adapted to desert life was the obvious choice.

CAMEL'S
CAMERA

Traditionally called "ships of the desert," camels are now vessels for photographing the world. Ten-year-old Raffia captured the **Liwa Desert** on a **camera attached to her hump**, becoming the first creature to assist Google in its quest to **map our planet**.

PEOPLE CAN USE STREET VIEW TO VISIT MUSEUMS AND EVEN SEE OLD EVENTS.

EXPLORERS USED STREET VIEW TO PHOTOGRAPH AN ACTIVE VOLCANO ON THE ISLAND COUNTRY OF VANUATU.

DAREDEVIL
CLIMBER

Spider-Man **scaling skyscrapers** is the stuff of superhero stories. But one Frenchman has **brought comic strips to life** with a series of incredible climbs. His **amazing antics** have led to both awards and arrests around the world.

Alain Robert has spent so long as a free climber, he can no longer fully straighten his fingers.

Free solo climber Alain Robert is seen here on his way up the Abu Dhabi Investment Authority (ADIA) Building, United Arab Emirates, in 2007. The skyscraper is 607 ft (185 m) high.

ALAIN ROBERT TRANSFORMED THE CEILING OF HIS FRENCH HOME INTO AN ARTIFICIAL CLIMBING WALL.

200 ROBERT HAS CLIMBED 200 OF TH WORLD'S TALLEST SKYSCRAPERS USING ONLY HIS BARE HANDS.

FAST FACTS

Sydney Opera House, 1997
ADIA Building, 2007
Eiffel Tower, 1996
Empire State Building, 1994
Burj Khalifa, 2011

Robert has conquered some of the world's most iconic buildings. In 2011, he climbed the world's tallest—the 2,716 ft (828 m) Burj Khalifa in Dubai. The climb was legal, but he had to use a safety harness to comply with regulations.

HEART-STOPPING SPORT

Meaning "free from aid," free solo climbing involves climbing without ropes or safety equipment. Climber extraordinaire Alain Robert has reached the summit of the world's tallest buildings, often using just a pair of climbing shoes and his bare hands. Some of his stunts have been authorized, but he has also been arrested many times for scaling buildings without permission.

BASE jumping is similar to free climbing— only in reverse and much quicker. Adrenaline enthusiasts leap from a fixed point, such as a cliff or building. They free fall before opening a parachute just in the nick of time to land safely.

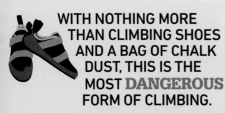

WITH NOTHING MORE THAN CLIMBING SHOES AND A BAG OF CHALK DUST, THIS IS THE MOST DANGEROUS FORM OF CLIMBING.

IN 2014, ALAN EUSTACE MADE A FREE-FALL JUMP FROM 135,899 FT (41,422 M) USING A SPACESUIT AND PARACHUTE.

AT THE TOP OF THEIR
GAME

This pair of aces were hitting high during their breathtaking **tennis match** on the **helipad of a seven-star hotel** in Dubai. Switzerland's Roger Federer played the US's Andre Agassi in a friendly game on the **world's highest court** in 2005.

Federer and Agassi were in training for the Dubai Duty Free Men's Championship when they gave this sky-high court a try.

IN 2017, DAREDEVIL NICK JACOBSEN LEAPT FROM THE HOTEL HELIPAD FOR A **KITEBOARDING** STUNT.

DJ DAVID GUETTA **PERFORMED** A LIVE-STREAMED SET FROM THE HELIPAD DURING THE COVID-19 PANDEMIC.

GAMES WITH ALTITUDE

In 2007, FIFA (soccer's governing body) banned international soccer matches at high altitude, but this rule was relaxed later. Playing at more than 8,200 ft (2,500 m) above sea level can affect a player's health. However, the thinner air also gives an advantage to players used to such conditions. This field in Switzerland is at 6,560 ft (2,000 m).

It is now possible to get married on the Burj Al Arab helipad—at vast expense.

FAST FACTS

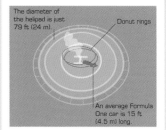

The diameter of the helipad is just 79 ft (24 m).

Donut rings

An average Formula One car is 15 ft (4.5 m) long.

The Burj Al Arab helipad has also been home to other sporting stunts. Formula One driver David Coulthard performed donuts in a race car in 2013—no mean feat in such a small space—and golfers Rory McIlroy and Tiger Woods have teed off from there.

The luxurious Burj Al Arab stands 1,053 ft (321 m) tall on a purpose-built island. Both players had the advantage when they saw the views of Dubai from the hotel's helipad, 692 ft (211 m) up. They smashed a few balls over the edge into the sea, but no one was eager to go and retrieve them!

IN 2022, ARTIST SACHA JAFRI DISPLAYED 30 **PAINTINGS** INSPIRED BY WORLD HERITAGE SITES ON THE HELIPAD.

IN 2023, A LIGHT AIRCRAFT BECAME THE FIRST **PLANE** TO LAND ON THE HELIPAD.

BASKET
BUILDING

Although it looks like the food hamper from a giants' picnic, this is a **basket-shaped building** open for business. Completed in 1997, the award-winning **architectural achievement** in Ohio was the brainchild of basket entrepreneur Dave Longaberger.

The building measures 190 ft (58 m) by 125 ft (38 m) at its base and 207 ft (63 m) by 141 ft (43 m) at the roof.

ADVERTISER'S DREAM

The US is crammed with business buildings designed to showcase the products on sale inside. Twistee Treat's ice-cream outlets are shaped like cones, Kansas City Library's parking garage (above) resembles a bookshelf, and Furnitureland in North Carolina looks like a chest of drawers.

THE BINOCULARS BUILDING IN CALIFORNIA HAS AN ENTRANCE IN THE SHAPE OF BINOCULARS.

A BUILDING IN SINGAPORE, CALLED THE HIVE, IS MADE TO LOOK LIKE PILES OF DIM SUM BASKETS STACKED TOGETHER.

Founder of the US's Longaberger Company, Dave Longaberger dreamed up the idea to house his offices inside the world's biggest basket. The building is a scaled-up version of the handcrafted maple wood baskets that were manufactured and distributed by Longaberger. Inside the lavish seven-story building in Newark, Ohio, are marble floors, cherry woodwork, and a sweeping staircase.

Stucco (a cement wall covering) covers the building's steel frame so that it closely resembles a handwoven basket.

FAST FACTS

The Basket Building weighs approximately 9,000 tons—the equivalent of 60 blue whales.

At 150 tons, the two handles alone weigh as much as one blue whale. They are heated in winter so they don't get iced up (which would make them even heavier).

There are 84 windows across all four sides of the building. The lights are left on at night so the whole structure lights up.

More than 4 million real Longaberger baskets would fit inside the building.

THE SANRIO STRAWBERRY HOUSE IN TOKYO, JAPAN, WAS BUILT IN 1984. IT LOOKS JUST LIKE A SUPERSIZE STRAWBERRY!

DINNY, A MODEL *BRONTOSAURUS* IN CALIFORNIA HAS A MUSEUM AND A GIFT SHOP INSIDE ITS TUMMY!

The **blue walls** are thought to **keep the town cool** in summer and **repel** insects.

These uneven wide steps and the pretty floral displays are typically Moroccan.

VENETIAN SPECTRUM

Burano is a multicolored island in Italy's Venetian lagoon. The houses are painted in glorious shades, with no two houses the same. The tradition originates with fishermen who painted their homes so they could spot them easily while fishing on the lagoon.

CHEFCHAOUEN GETS A FRESH COAT OF **PAINT** TWICE A YEAR TO KEEP ITS COLOR.

EVEN **TAXIS** IN CHEFCHAOUEN ARE PAINTED A BRILLIANT BLUE.

SMALL TOWN
BLUES

Known as the **Blue Pearl**, Chefchaouen in Morocco is truly blue. All the buildings in its medina (old town) are **painted blue**, contrasting with the arid **Rif Mountains** surrounding the town. There is a religious meaning behind the **blue hue**.

First built as a 15th-century fortress, Chefchaouen turned blue in the 1930s, thanks to local Jewish people. In Judaism, blue represents God, heaven, and sky. Ancient Jewish teachings state that dyeing thread with *tekhelet* (a natural indigo dye) would keep God in mind, a tradition that lives on in today's blue buildings.

FAST FACTS

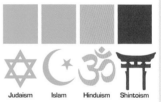

| Judaism | Islam | Hinduism | Shintoism |

Judaism is not the only religion to favor a particular color. For Muslims, the color green symbolizes nature and life, while for Hindus, saffron (an orange-yellow color) represents purity. Shinto temples in Japan are often painted red—a color associated with purification and protection from evil spirits.

MULES ARE OFTEN USED BY TOURISTS AND TO TRANSPORT GOODS AROUND THE TOWN.

THE PEOPLE OF **BURANO** ARE TOLD WHEN TO PAINT THEIR HOMES AND WHICH COLORS TO USE.

Peculiar plants

Why does the dragon's blood tree bleed and the Cannonball tree fire fruit? Take a stroll through Earth's boundless botanical garden and get to the roots of its secrets. Along the way, encounter the grandest growers, biggest bloomers, freakiest flowers, and stinkiest species.

As bark peels off at different times and in different places, the rainbow eucalyptus tree becomes a kaleidoscope of color. This fierce grower doubles in size each year until it reaches the dizzy height of 200 ft (60 m).

FLEETING
FLOWER

The supersize Titan arum is an **absolute showstopper** of the horticultural world, taking many **years to flower**. Botanists wait with baited breath for this unpredictable giant to bloom in **brief but breathtaking** glory.

The fleshy spadix heats up as the plant flowers and emits a powerful odor.

The protective spathe unfurls to reveal rings of flowers at the base of the spadix.

The flower emerges from a huge tuber (underground stem) that can weigh more than 154 lb (70 kg).

POISON IN PARADISE

While Titan arum is smelly but harmless, *Daphne mezereum* is the opposite. Nicknamed the paradise plant, this species produces fragrant flowers, hiding the fact that it is deadly poisonous. Swallowing any part of this plant would lead to sudden sickness or even death.

23 WHEN A TITAN ARUM DOES NOT FLOWER, IT PRODUCES A LEAF MEASURING **23 FT** (7 M).

RED FRUITS THAT GROW ON THE TITAN ARUM ARE DISPERSED BY THE **RHINOCEROS HORNBILL**.

This rare species grows in Sumatran rainforests, but its spectacular size has made it a favorite at botanical gardens. Its single flower head consists of a spadix (flower-bearing spike) surrounded by a leaflike spathe. Flowering occurs only occasionally and lasts just days, accompanied by the rancid smell of rotting meat. When the flower dies, a single leaf the size of a small tree takes its place. This builds up food stores so the plant will eventually flower again.

The **flower head emerging from the tuber adds 4 in (10 cm) to** its height **per day**.

FAST FACTS

The sizable Titan arum flower is not a single flower; it is an inflorescence, or flower spike, bearing hundreds of flowers.

The century plant has a taller flower spike than the Titan arum, which it sends up every 20–30 years.

The talipot palm has the largest flower spike of all. Its flowers form a 26 ft (8 m) structure on top of the tree, which itself can be up to 82 ft (25 m) tall.

Titan arum

Century plant

Talipot palm

| 10 ft (3 m) | 29 ft (9 m) | 82 ft + 26 ft (25 m + 8 m) |

A TITAN ARUM THAT IS GROWN FROM A SEED TAKES UP TO **10 YEARS** TO BLOOM.

THE PLANT'S STRONG STENCH ATTRACTS POLLINATORS, SUCH AS **CARRION BEETLES** AND FLESH FLIES.

HOT
LIPS

This plant may look like it is puckering up for a **saucy smooch**, but it's really saving all its love for **hummingbirds** and **butterflies**. The vibrant liplike parts are **specialized leaves** designed to draw these feeders to its **sweet nectar**.

SNAPDRAGON SKULLS

Blooming in the sunshine, snapdragon flowers are colorful and beautiful, but things take a sinister turn when their seed pods dry out to resemble tiny skulls.

In this gap, the plant will grow its small white flowers. As butterflies and hummingbirds land on the flowers to drink nectar, they transfer pollen from flower to flower. This is essential for the plant's reproduction.

13 A HOT LIPS PLANT CAN GROW TO DIZZY HEIGHTS OF UP TO **13 FT** (4 M).

PEOPLE SUFFERING FROM SNAKE BITES IN NICARAGUA USE THIS PLANT TO **RELIEVE** HARMFUL SIDE EFFECTS.

In **Central America**, this attractive plant is often given as a **token of love**.

FAST FACTS

The hot lips plant is not the only plant to resemble something else. The yellow, orange, and red flowers of the flame lily resemble a roaring fire. The bleeding heart has bright pink, heart-shaped flowers, while the bird of paradise plant looks just like its namesake, complete with colorful plumage.

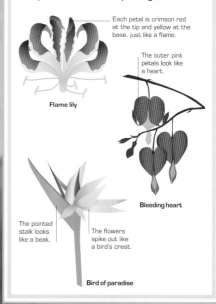

Each petal is crimson red at the tip and yellow at the base, just like a flame.

Flame lily

The outer pink petals look like a heart.

Bleeding heart

The pointed stalk looks like a beak.

The flowers spike out like a bird's crest.

Bird of paradise

Palicourea elata **is the scientific name** for the hot lips plant, which flowers in the humid forests of Central and South America. Called bracts, the glossy red leaves are the perfect color to catch the eye of pollinators because butterfly and hummingbird eyes are very attracted to red light.

The plant's "lips" measure about 2 in (5 cm) from top to bottom.

THE PLANT IS **ENDANGERED** AS LARGE PARTS OF ITS FOREST HABITAT HAVE BEEN CLEARED FOR FARMLAND.

A SUCCULENT CALLED **STRING OF DOLPHINS** IS NAMED AFTER ITS CURVY LEAVES THAT LOOK LIKE LEAPING DOLPHINS.

POSTURING
PETALS

Some flowers can make you **look twice**. Although their **real identities** are floral, they resemble something **entirely different**.

Monkey business
The flowers of *Dracula simia*, or the monkey orchid, are a dead ringer for a mini monkey face. Preferring high altitude habitats in Ecuador and Peru, this unique flower has also been grown in captivity by orchid experts.

THE EVERGREEN **ALPINE FLOWER**, DARWIN'S SLIPPER, LOOKS LIKE AN ALIEN OR A PENGUIN.

NATIVE TO AUSTRALIA THE *CALEANA MAJOR* IS A **SMALL ORCHID** THAT RESEMBLES A DUCK IN FLIGHT.

Budding baby
The *Anguloa uniflora* is a short orchid native to northern South America, with each flower mimicking a baby wrapped up in swaddling cloth. The creamy, scented petals open in the summer months.

Buzzy bloomer
At first glance, this looks like bees drawing nectar from flowers. But look again. Growing around the Mediterranean and Middle East, this is the woodcock bee-orchid, a flower that closely resembles a bee.

Parrot petals
Native to Myanmar, Thailand, and India, the rare *Impatiens psittacina* is better known as the parrot flower because its pretty pastel petals look just like a parrot in flight.

THE **FLOWERS** OF THE *ARISTOLOCHIA* PLANT LOOK JUST LIKE THE *STAR WARS* VILLAIN DARTH VADER.

AN IMAGE OF *SENECIO PEREGRINUS*, WHICH HAS LEAVES SHAPED LIKE DOLPHINS, RECEIVED 10,500 **TWEETS** IN 2017.

ATTACK OF THE
KILLER PLANTS

There are more than 600 species of **carnivorous plants** on Earth, but nature's most famous meat-muncher is the **Venus flytrap**. These jaws of death prey on **vulnerable insects**—and when they **snap shut**, there's no escape.

Unscrupulous collectors dig up the wild plants, putting the Venus flytrap under threat.

An unsuspecting cricket moves closer to the sweet nectar secreted from the Venus flytrap's open leaves.

EACH TRAP IS A **SINGLE LEAF** FOLDED IN HALF.

THE PLANT PREYS MOSTLY ON **ANTS AND SPIDERS** ALONG WITH SOME BEETLES AND FLYING INSECTS.

FAST FACTS

The Venus flytrap's lightning reflexes are not well understood, but they may be the result of electrical impulses. When the trigger hairs are touched, a signal causes water to move rapidly between the leaf's cells so that the cells on the outside of the leaf swell up, making the trap snap shut.

Brushing a hair stimulates a tiny electrical impulse but not enough to shut the trap.

Touching a second hair increases the charge and triggers the trap.

Cells on the outside of the leaf swell with water and the trap snaps shut.

Formally known as *Dionaea muscipula*, this predatory plant grows in the wetlands of North and South Carolina. A carnivorous plant is one that lures, traps, kills, and digests its prey, and the Venus flytrap does all of these in quick succession, thanks to its special touch-sensitive leaves. Trigger hairs on the leaves detect prey but withstand false alarms such as drops of rain.

Snap! The leaves close tight around the cricket. Glands on the leaf release digestive fluids that break down the cricket's soft tissues, then absorb the nutritious insect soup.

The cricket touches trigger hairs on the leaves, and the plant's touch-sensitive mechanism responds instantly.

MIGHTY MOUSETRAP

One of the largest carnivorous plants in the world is *Nepenthes attenboroughii*, native to the Philippines. Reaching a height of 4.9 ft (1.5 m), its leafy jaws can trap and digest mice and rats.

A VENUS FLYTRAP **SNAPS SHUT** ONLY IF AN INSECT TOUCHES ITS TRIGGER HAIRS TWO TIMES IN 20 SECONDS.

HAVING DIGESTED ITS MEAL, THE LEAF **OPENS AGAIN** AFTER ABOUT A WEEK.

TREE ART

Tree shaping transforms plants into living art. Bending, weaving, and twisting help these sculptures take shape. The art form takes advantage of a process called inosculation—where tissue from two different plants, or parts of a plant that are touching, knits itself together.

TREE
BRIDGES

In the **forests of northeastern India**, rivers and streams are crossed using structures crafted from **ancient rubber fig trees**. Forged by tangled roots and vines, these living tree bridges are both a **natural wonder** and an engineering masterclass.

The roots of the *Ficus elastica*, a type of rubber fig tree, twist into strong lattices.

100 THERE ARE MORE THAN **100 LIVING TREE BRIDGES** IN MEGHALAYA.

IN THE PAST, LOCAL PEOPLE USED TREE BRIDGES TO TAKE **BROOM GRASS** TO CITIES FOR TRADE.

Some of Cherrapunji's tree bridges are thought to be more than 500 years old.

Cherrapunji in the Indian state of Meghalaya is one of the world's wettest places, so normal wooden structures would rot and break. Living bridges avoid this problem, enabling these children to get to school. By carefully guiding the strong, thick tree roots across rivers and voids, local Khasi people have grown permanent crossings that only get stronger over time. Patience and planning are required; they take 10 to 15 years to grow.

FAST FACTS

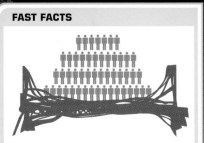

Some tree bridges are up to 100 ft (30 m) long and can support the weight of 50 people or more at once. Local people use hollowed-out tree trunks to guide new roots into position and ensure the structure is strong.

TREE BRIDGES ARE HOME TO VARIOUS TYPES OF BIRDS, INSECTS, AND MAMMALS.

174

AT 174 FT (53 M) LONG, RANGTHYLLIANG IN MEGHALAYA, IS THE WORLD'S LONGEST TREE BRIDGE.

TREE OF
BLOOD

It can't fly and it doesn't breathe fire, but the **dragon's blood tree** can make one extraordinary claim to fame. The **bark of the tree bleeds**, leading to its use in magic and **medicine** since ancient times.

The dragon's blood tree (*Dracaena cinnabari*) has an unusual appearance, with branches like bony fingers reaching up to a crown of evergreen leaves. The blood-red sap is secreted naturally from cracks and cuts in the trunk. Harvesters open the existing fissures to collect the oozing sap, which has a variety of uses.

Legend claims the "blood" is an effective ingredient in love spells.

This slow-growing species is unique to the islands of Socotra in the Indian Ocean.

NEW BLOOD

The deep-red sap of the dragon's blood tree is an effective ingredient in dyes, varnish, adhesive, and incense. It has also been successful in treating cuts, bites, burns, and sores because the resin's healing properties reduce redness and swelling.

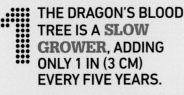 THE DRAGON'S BLOOD TREE IS A SLOW GROWER, ADDING ONLY 1 IN (3 CM) EVERY FIVE YEARS.

 MANY REPTILES, INCLUDING THE DRAGON TREE HALF-TOED GECKO, LIVE IN THESE TREES.

The dragon's blood tree grows up to 33 ft (10 m) in height.

FAST FACTS

Long, waxy leaves catch droplets of water from clouds of mist.

Water droplets run down the branches and trunk to the roots.

Although the dragon's blood tree looks like an umbrella, it is designed to collect, rather than repel, water. The long, waxy leaves gather moisture from the air and transport it down to the branches, trunk, and roots, enabling the tree to survive in Socotra's hot and dry climate.

600

THE TREE HAS A LIFE SPAN OF MORE THAN 600 YEARS.

THE TREE BLOOMS FRAGRANT WHITE FLOWERS IN LATE WINTER OR EARLY SPRING.

TOP
TRUNKS

Some trees are not just **part of the scenery**—they define the landscape with their **bizarre beauty**.

Tree of life
A prehistoric wonder in its native Africa, Australia, and Madagascar, the baobab is called "the tree of life." It can store huge amounts of water in its swollen trunk, enabling it to survive seasonal droughts.

BAOBAB TREES BLOOM ONCE A YEAR AND THE FLOWERS LAST JUST ONE NIGHT.

GINKGO TREES EXISTED BEFORE DINOSAURS, AND ONE SPECIES—*GINKGO BILOBA*—STILL GROWS TODAY.

Desert roots
The skinny and spiny Boojum tree soars above the other vegetation of the Sonoran Desert in Mexico. At more than 50 ft (15 m), this species grows taller whenever there is rainfall, though it can survive for years on very little rainfall.

Timber tunnel
The US is famous for its drive-through destinations, even including a tree! A giant redwood named Chandelier Tree in Leggett, California, has a tunnel carved through its big base. Cars can pass through once a park-entry fee has been paid.

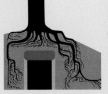

WHEN CHERRY TREES FLOWER IN JAPAN, IT'S TIME TO CELEBRATE! THIS TRADITION BEGAN 1,200 YEARS AGO.

AS ITS NAME SUGGESTS, THE STRANGLER FIG TREE WRAPS ITS ROPELIKE ROOTS ON ANYTHING IT COMES ACROSS, INCLUDING BUILDINGS.

ARMED AND
DECIDUOUS

There's no better protected tree than the **Cannonball**. This **gargantuan grower** is found in South American forests and **attacks without warning**. Avoid being in the firing line when its weighty fruits **blast off**.

The tree towers up to **115 ft (35 m)** and each fruit can weigh about **6 lb (3 kg)**.

A member of the Brazil nut family, the Cannonball tree's proper name is *Couroupita guianensis*. Although it is native to the rainforests of the Guianas (an area of northeastern South America), it is cultivated in different tropical and subtropical areas around the world. The tree has sweet-smelling flowers that are used in perfumes and cosmetics. Its heavy fruit look like rusty cannonballs and when ripe, they fall to the ground and smash open with a bang. Locals use the fruit shells to craft containers and utensils.

TREE TREATMENT

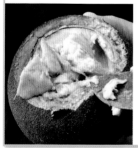

The Cannonball's bark, leaves, and fruit have been used in medicine for centuries. The beneficial bark is said to prevent colds and have antiseptic properties, while the leaves treat various skin diseases. The stinky fruit is used as a natural disinfectant for open wounds.

THOUSANDS OF **FLOWERS** COVER THESE TREES, BUT EACH FLOWER LASTS ONLY A DAY.

550

THE **BIGGEST** CANNONBALL FRUIT CONTAINS AS MANY AS 550 SEEDS.

The flesh of the large, round fruit is edible, but it gives off an overpowering stench. ......

FAST FACTS

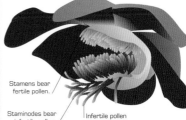

Stamens bear fertile pollen.

Staminodes bear infertile pollen.

Infertile pollen attracts pollinators such as bees and bats.

Flowers of trees in the Brazil nut family have a unique structure. The fertile stamens form a fleshy ring, with a secondary mass of infertile stamens, called staminodes, making a kind of hood. Only the strongest pollinators—large bees or some bats—can lift the hood and collect the infertile pollen. As they do so, they brush the stamens, carrying the fertile pollen to the next flower they visit.

MANY ANIMALS, INCLUDING PACAS, EAT THE FRUIT AND HELP SPREAD THE SEEDS.

THE FRUITS CAN BE USED TO MAKE AN INDIGO PIGMENT FOR DYEING CLOTH.

ALGAE
ATTACK!

China's **Yellow Sea** often turns green, caused by massive **algae growths**. Since 2007, algae have swamped the waters every summer. The 2013 **bumper bloom** covered a whopping **11,158 sq miles** (28,900 sq km).

The species of algae—*Enteromorpha prolifera*—is not toxic, so swimmers and waders fearlessly jump in.

Eating this type of algae can help improve skin and lower blood pressure.

A MASS OF **SARGASSUM SEAWEED** FLOATING IN THE ATLANTIC OCEAN IS THE LARGEST MACROALGAE BLOOM IN THE WORLD.

IN 2014, A TOXIC ALGAE BLOOM IN LAKE ERIE LED TO A BAN ON THE USE OF **TAP WATER** IN OHIO.

FAST FACTS

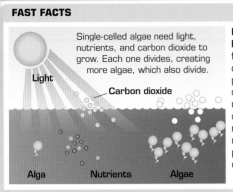

Single-celled algae need light, nutrients, and carbon dioxide to grow. Each one divides, creating more algae, which also divide.

Light

Carbon dioxide

Alga   Nutrients   Algae

Harmful algal blooms (HABs) form where colonies of sea-inhabiting plants, called algae, develop at a rapid rate, causing devastation to local marine life. In the right conditions, a population of algae can double in hours.

Despite the fun and frolics on the beach at Qingdao in the eastern Shandong province, this thick covering of algae stops sunlight and oxygen from penetrating the water, which suffocates sealife. Scientists don't know why the tide has turned green, but they agree that the carpet of algae comes from an ecosystem imbalance, and is probably the result of human activity, such as agricultural and industrial pollution.

More than 8,085 tons of algae had to be removed from the beaches by city officials using bulldozers.

BRING ON THE BLUES

Electric blue algal blooms off the coast of Hong Kong look brilliantly bioluminescent, but what lies beneath is toxic pollution. Harmful *Noctiluca scintillans*, or sea sparkle, is flourishing because of excessive fertilizer and sewage. This devastates the landscape, killing local marine life.

THERE ARE AT LEAST 300 HARMFUL ALGAL SPECIES WORLDWIDE.

MACROALGAE, INCLUDING THE RED SEAWEED NORI, HAS BEEN USED IN FOOD FOR THOUSANDS OF YEARS.

FOUL
FLOWER

Even the greenest fingers stop at the **corpse flower**. The biggest bloomer on Earth, this species is also the **stinkiest**, pervading the atmosphere with the **stench of rotten flesh**. What a relief that it's one of the world's **rarest flowers**!

ITSY-BITSY BLOOM

At the other end of the floral spectrum is the Asian watermeal plant, or *Wolffia globosa*. Smaller than a grain of rice, this green grower is the world's smallest flowering plant, and can be found floating in streams and ponds.

The corpse flower features in Indonesian tourist brochures as a symbol of the region's vibrant rainforests.

STUDIES SUGGEST THAT *RAFFLESIA ARNOLDII* SWAPS GENES WITH ITS HOST PLANT.

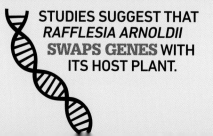

THE PLANT IS POLLINATED BY CARRION FLIES, TRICKED INTO VISITING THE FLOWER BY THE SMELL OF ROTTING MEAT.

Each flower is made up of red lobes with white spots, resting on a cup-like structure.

FAST FACTS

The diameter of the largest *Rafflesia* flowers is equivalent to half the height of a man.

Though other flowers have larger clusters of flower heads, the corpse flower is the largest single flower. It is about 1 m (3 ft) wide and can weigh 10 kg (22 lb).

The flower buds are used in traditional medicine to aid recovery after childbirth.

Rafflesia arnoldii, **as it is formally known**, uses disgusting odours to lure flies and other insects to pollinate the plant. Native to the rainforests of Borneo and Sumatra, it takes up to 10 months to bloom fully before the flower dies a week later. The plant has no leaves or stem, but lives as a parasite inside a host plant, hidden from view until the flower bud bursts through and the giant bloom unfurls.

A SINGLE CORPSE FLOWER CAN WEIGH AS MUCH AS A CAR TYRE.

IT WOULD TAKE ABOUT 5,000 ASIAN WATERMEAL PLANTS TO FILL A THIMBLE.

FREAKY
FLORA

The most **incredible plants** can grow from a humble seed. Around the world some **dramatically different** forms have **taken root**.

Size matters
The giant water lily grows year-round in South America. With leaves 8 ft (2.4 m) across, it can carry up to 100 lb (45 kg) in weight, so these pigeons pose no problem.

Tree tumbo
Considered by many to be an ugly and unruly plant, the tree tumbo plant just keeps on growing. It can survive for 1,500 years in parts of the Namib Desert.

LEAVES OF THE GIANT WATER LILY ARE STRONG ENOUGH TO SUPPORT THE WEIGHT OF A **NEWBORN BABY**.

SPIKES ON THE UNDERSIDES OF GIANT WATER LILY LEAVES PROTECT SMALL FISH AND AMPHIBIANS FROM PREDATORS.

Monkey cup

The *Nepenthes* pitcher plant, which grows in Australia, South East Asia, and Madagascar, is known as "monkey cup" because it was once believed that monkeys liked the fluid inside its pitchers. Insects fall into this carnivorous vine's tropical trap in pursuit of nectar but end up getting eaten themselves.

Hanging bangers

The *Kigelia africana*, or Sausage tree, can be seen across Africa's wetter regions. This whopper species grows to about 66 ft (20 m) in height and has strange sausage-like fruits that are around 3 ft (1 m) long.

THE LITHOPS PLANT FROM SOUTHERN AFRICA LOOKS JUST LIKE SMALL STONES, SO ANIMALS RARELY EAT THEM.

THE GHOST PLANT, *MONOTROPA UNIFLORA*, GETS ITS NAME FROM ITS SPOOKY WHITE COLOR. IT TURNS BLACK WHEN PICKED.

OUT OF
THE BLUE

The picture-perfect islands of the **Maldives** are famed for white beaches lapped by the Indian Ocean. But Vaadhoo Island is most breathtaking after dark when single-celled algae (phytoplankton) turn the water electric blue. In this natural phenomenon, the **sparkling sea** appears to **reflect the starry night**.

> Many sea creatures feed on phytoplankton, including whales, sea snails, and jellyfish.

THE SMALL **FIREFLY SQUID** LIGHTS UP THE OCEAN WITH ITS MULTIPLE EYE AND ARM LIGHTS.

THE **KITEFIN SHARK** GLOWS BRILLIANTLY BLUE AND IS THE LARGEST BIOLUMINESCENT VERTEBRATE.

Microscopic marine microbes called phytoplankton live in the sea. When they are disturbed, a chemical reaction called bioluminescence (biological light) takes place—a flashing blue light is produced by the phytoplankton. This usually happens at sea when a ship or large fish disturbs the water. Vaadhoo is unusual because bioluminescence occurs on the shore.

Each wave releases a flash of glowing blue in the many millions of phytoplankton washed up on the sand.

FAST FACTS

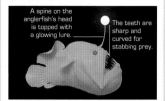

A spine on the anglerfish's head is topped with a glowing lure.

The teeth are sharp and curved for stabbing prey.

Many deep-sea creatures have evolved to produce their own bright light in the darkness. The anglerfish uses a bioluminescent "lantern" to tempt prey. Dangling from a spine on the fish's head, this lantern houses bacteria that use chemicals produced by the fish to glow.

GLOW IN THE DARK

The Waitomo Caves in New Zealand are a haven for glowworms. This unique species—*Arachnocampa luminosa*—produces a striking light in the darkness. Boat trips into the caves take tourists to visit the glimmering glowworms.

SOME MUSHROOMS CONTAIN LIGHT-EMITTING COMPOUNDS TO ATTRACT INSECTS.

EACH SPECIES OF FIREFLY HAS ITS OWN DISTINCTIVE PATTERN OF LIGHTS.

Curious creatures

The animal kingdom is home to some truly fabulous fauna, slithering and sliding, racing and wriggling, and plunging and pouncing in every corner of nature's rich theater. Witness a breathtaking display of animal magic, with showstopping performances from dancing arachnids, acrobatic mammals, and reptile impersonators.

Poison dart frogs come in a spectrum of startling shades, sending a clear warning to predators to keep away. This brilliant blue species was discovered only in 1968 and is one of the world's only blue creatures.

CRAB
ARMY

Every year up to **100 million red crabs** inhabiting Australia's **Christmas Island** migrate from their forest home to the Indian Ocean. This convoy of crustaceans travels 5.5 miles (9 km) with **one sole goal**—reproduction.

Christmas Island red crabs **can measure up to 4.5 in (11.5 cm) across.**

BAT CAVE

Another huge concentration of creatures can be found at Bracken Cave in the US, home to the world's largest bat colony. About 20 million bats exit the cave every day at dusk searching for insects to feed on—one of nature's most amazing aerial sights.

Amorous male crabs will fight each other during the annual migration, competing for the attention of the females.

RED CRABS CROSS ROADS, BRIDGES, AND EVEN TRAIN TRACKS ON THEIR JOURNEY.

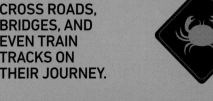

ROADS ARE SHUT AND **SPECIAL CROSSINGS** ARE BUILT TO KEEP THE CRABS SAFE AS THEY TRAVEL.

FAST FACTS

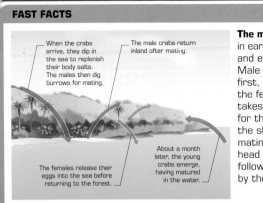

When the crabs arrive, they dip in the sea to replenish their body salts. The males then dig burrows for mating.

The male crabs return inland after mating.

The females release their eggs into the sea before returning to the forest.

About a month later, the young crabs emerge, having matured in the water.

The migration starts in early November and ends in January. Male crabs set off first, followed by the female crabs. It takes about a week for them to reach the shore. After mating, the males head back inland, followed soon after by the females.

The crabs are making their way to the sea. Mating takes place on the shore because the larval form of the crab has primitive gills that function only in water. Female crabs release eggs into the sea. The larvae hatch and grow in the water for about a month before congregating at the shore, ready to become mini air-breathing crabs. The tiny baby crabs then head back to the forest.

Male crabs reach the beach first and dig the burrows where mating will take place.

 A FEMALE RED CRAB CARRIES HER EGGS FOR ABOUT **TWO WEEKS** IN A BROOD POUCH BENEATH HER BODY.

 THE VAST MAJORITY OF BABY CRABS ARE AN EASY TARGET FOR **PREDATORS**, INCLUDING SHARKS AND MANTA RAYS.

JUMBO
JITTERS

It's every elephant's worst nightmare—just when you're chilling out by a watering hole, a **swarm of thousands of squawking birds** comes and spoils the serenity. **Overwhelmed by the frenzy**, this jumbo soon backed away.

Red-billed quelea are the world's most plentiful wild birds, with an adult breeding population of about 1.5 billion.

RED-BILLED QUELEA CAN BUILD UP TO 6,000 NESTS IN A SINGLE TREE.

MILLIONS OF THESE BIRDS MAKE UP A FLOCK AND CAN TAKE **HOURS** TO PASS ONE SPOT.

These tiny birds are red-billed quelea. They weigh just 0.5–0.7 oz (15–20 g) each, but their huge number meant the total weight suddenly snapped a tree branch at Kenya's Satao Camp water hole in 2012. Taking to the skies, their deafening call and ferocious flapping of wings was too much for the big-eared elephant, who made a hasty retreat.

FAST FACTS

Flocks of red-billed quelea are a menace for farmers in Africa. One swarm can eat several fields of grain (up to 55 tons) in a day—about the weight of seven elephants.

The **African elephant** is the world's **largest living land animal.**

SCAREDY CATS

Despite being king of the beasts, lions have also been known to scare easily. A pack of lions was seen stalking an adult and baby giraffe in Kenya's Maasai Mara. Fearing for her offspring's safety, the giraffe charged, and the pack ran away.

FEEDING TIME IS AN ACROBATIC AFFAIR AS BIRDS AT THE REAR "LEAPFROG" TO THE FRONT TO FIND A NEW FEEDING SPOT.

LOCUSTS, FISH, AND SNAKES ARE ALSO KNOWN TO CROWD TOGETHER TO BREED, MIGRATE, OR HUNT.

DREAM
TEAMS

Teaming up works wonders in the animal kingdom. From aerial attacks to making mounds, there is definitely **strength in numbers**.

Golden jelly
Jellyfish Lake sits on a remote island of the Palau archipelago in the Pacific Ocean. This saltwater lake is the perfect home for millions of harmless jellyfish because there are plenty of algae to feed on and no predators to avoid.

 **GOLDEN JELLYFISH** MIGRATE ACROSS JELLYFISH LAKE DAILY, FOLLOWING THE LIGHT FROM THE SUN.

SOME OF THE MASSIVE **TERMITE MOUNDS** ARE AS OLD AS THE PYRAMIDS OF EGYPT.

Spanish swarm
In 2004, the skies over the Spanish island of Fuerteventura were plagued by swarms of pink locusts from Africa. Their collective power destroyed crops in some African countries, before 100 million of them flew on to Fuerteventura.

Wonder weavers
Named after their huge woven nests standing up to 13 ft (4 m) tall, sociable weaver birds of southern Africa work together to gather twigs, stems, and grass for their carefully constructed homes.

Massive mounds
There's no slacking in the termite team. Like ants and bees, this insect knows the power of many. Termite builders in Africa, Australia, and South America (above) create enormous mounds that are up to 26 ft (8 m) tall. These homes can take five years to complete.

400 THE GIANT NEST OF A WEAVER BIRD CAN PROVIDE A HOME FOR UP TO **400 BIRDS**.

IN ONE DAY, A SWARM OF 80 MILLION **LOCUSTS** CAN EAT AS MUCH FOOD AS 35,000 PEOPLE.

MARATHON
MIGRATION

It's a journey that would have most of us reaching for our passports, but **monarch butterflies** cover **3,000 miles (4,800 km)** on their annual flight from **Canada to Mexico**. The skies fill with **millions of monarchs** in the world's longest **insect migration**.

Monarch butterflies travel up to **100 miles (160 km) per day** on their journey south.

SUPPORTING THE SPECIES

Monarch butterflies lay their eggs only on milkweed plants because they are the sole food of the newly hatched larvae. However, herbicide use has decreased the number of milkweed plants in North America. Conservationists are encouraging people to plant milkweeds at home, to create the habitat the monarchs need to survive.

THE MONARCH IS THE ONLY BUTTERFLY THAT MAKES A **TWO-WAY** MIGRATION.

AFTER THEY ARE BORN, MONARCH BUTTERFLIES GROW **2,700 TIMES** IN SIZE IN THE FIRST FEW WEEKS.

Monarch butterflies can't survive the cold Canadian winter, so they fly south to warmer climes. Most monarchs live for a maximum of eight weeks, but the generation that hatches at the end of the Canadian summer is different. Instead of mating and dying, they put all their energy into the migration and can live for up to eight months. After spending the winter in Mexico, the migrating generation reproduce and their offspring make the journey back to Canada.

In Mexico, the monarch butterflies roost on the trunks and branches of fir trees to conserve energy.

FAST FACTS

Like all butterflies, monarchs go through four distinct stages in their life cycle. They are laid as eggs, which hatch into larvae, or caterpillars. The larva feeds, shedding its skin four or more times as its body gets bigger.

Egg

Larva

Imago

Pupa

The larva then becomes a pupa, or chrysalis. Inside the pupa, the larva turns into an imago—an adult butterfly. The whole process from egg to butterfly is called metamorphosis.

The butterflies return to the same small area and often the exact same trees as previous generations.

A MONARCH CATERPILLAR CAN EAT AN ENTIRE MILKWEED LEAF IN LESS THAN FIVE MINUTES.

MONARCHS FLY AT SPEEDS OF 12 MPH (19 KM/H).

WORLD'S WILD
WEBS

If **millions of spiders** congregate in one place, they can work as a team, spinning **enormous sheet webs** that **cover trees**, **hedges**, and **fields**. These wonder weavers transform the landscape with their **intricate designs**.

FAST FACTS

The spider with the longest legs is a species discovered in a cave in Laos in 2001—the giant huntsman spider. It measures 12 in (30 cm) from the tip of one leg to the tip of its opposite leg. The biggest spider by weight is the Goliath birdeater, a species of South American tarantula that weighs up to 6 oz (170 g).

12 in
(30 cm)
ruler

Giant
huntsman
spider

These webs are so dense that trees appear to be covered in nets.

When water levels rose several feet above Sindh's normal levels, wildlife headed for the trees to survive.

IN 2010, THE SUPERSIZE SPIDER WEBS TRAPPED MOSQUITOES, HELPING TO REDUCE MOSQUITO-TRANSMITTED DISEASES IN SINDH.

60

A SPIDER CAN WEAVE AN ENTIRE WEB IN 60 MINUTES.

Spiders **made these webs when a** decade's worth **of rain dropped** on Sindh in a week**.**

In 2010, many trees were blanketed by giant webs in Sindh, Pakistan, when heavy monsoon rains flooded large areas. Spiders and other web-spinning creatures living on the ground had to seek shelter. They climbed trees to escape the flood waters, and their handiwork was visible for all to see.

ANIMAL ORACLES

Some creatures can predict natural disasters. Birds take flight when they sense a storm coming, and researchers in Florida found that sharks swim into deeper water before a hurricane.

THE WORLD'S LARGEST WEB, AT 82 FT (25 M) ACROSS, WAS MADE BY A DARWIN'S BARK SPIDER.

1,000

THE SILK PRODUCED BY SPIDERS IS 1,000 TIMES THINNER THAN HUMAN HAIR.

STRUTTING
SPIDER

Australia's **peacock spider** makes all the right **moves** in a bid to impress the ladies. Getting into the groove is easy with **eight legs** and a multicolored stomach flap to shake.

Peacock spiders have eight **eyes** and can see fine details in color from yards away.

FAST FACTS

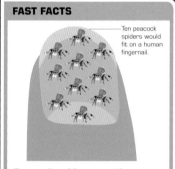

Ten peacock spiders would fit on a human fingernail.

Peacock spiders are tiny— adults grow to only about 4 mm long. Despite this, these aptly named jumping spiders are capable of pouncing more than 20 times their body length.

A PEACOCK SPIDER'S CENTRAL EYES COVER HALF OF ITS HEAD.

UNLIKE OTHER SPIDERS, THE PEACOCK SPIDER USUALLY HUNTS DURING THE DAY.

The colorful stomach flap of the male spider is lifted like a fan during the courtship dance. At other times, it remains folded away out of sight.

The courtship dance of the male peacock spider involves a series of attention-grabbing jumps, sways, and struts to attract partners. His colors and moves are studied by the female before she decides if he is a suitable mate. If she isn't interested, she may attack and eat her suitor instead!

After mating, the peacock spider will get up and moving again to find more females.

This spider gets its name from the equally flashy peacock bird.

PLUMAGE OF PARADISE

The mating efforts of the male Vogelkop superb bird of paradise are hard to ignore. The bird is transformed by showcasing his big, brilliant-blue frontage before he performs an impressive courtship dance. His performance must be perfect to win over the drably colored female.

THE MALE BOWERBIRD BUILDS NESTLIKE STRUCTURES AND DECORATES THEM WITH SHINY OBJECTS TO ATTRACT FEMALES.

THE MALE AND FEMALE GREAT CRESTED GREBE DANCE TOGETHER IN THEIR SO-CALLED "WATER BALLET."

BLOATED
BLOODSUCKERS

Ticks are the **vampires** of the bug brigade, gorging on blood for survival. The **Rocky Mountain wood tick** swells to many times its original size after a grand feast. **Bloated on blood**, the wood tick drops off its weakened host.

At home in the higher ground of Colorado, the Rocky Mountain wood tick (*Dermacentor andersoni*) is a three-host species. It feeds three times in its three-year lifetime—as a newly hatched larva, as a nymph, and as an adult. While small creatures suffice for its first two feeds, this tick's last supper features deer, sheep, or even people!

An adult wood tick can **live for** about 600 days **without feeding.**

The adult wood tick is armed and dangerous, with a hard shell and a ruthless bite.

FAST FACTS

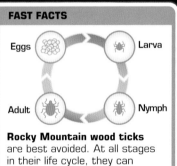

Eggs — Larva

Adult — Nymph

Rocky Mountain wood ticks are best avoided. At all stages in their life cycle, they can transmit tick-borne diseases to humans, cats, and dogs. In most cases, the victim has just 24 hours to remove the tick from the skin (by grasping it with blunt tweezers) before the body is infected.

Before

TICKS TYPICALLY **CLING TO PLANTS,** WAITING TO LATCH ONTO PASSING CREATURES.

TICKS ARE HIGHLY SENSITIVE, DETECTING THEIR PREY BY **SCENT OR BODY HEAT.**

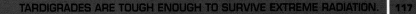

The tick feeds on its host and grows until it is fully engorged with blood.

Ticks are arachnids— closely related to spiders. There are up to 900 species of ticks.

After

MIGHTY MICROBUG

The tardigrade is only 1 mm long, but virtually indestructible. Dropped in boiling water or left in frozen ice, this little fighter won't flinch. Remove its water supply for a decade or launch it into space, and there's still no harm done.

ROCKY MOUNTAIN WOOD TICKS HAVE A LIFE SPAN OF UP TO 3 YEARS.

TICKS USE PINCER-LIKE JAWS TO PUNCTURE THE SKIN OF THEIR PREY AND SUCK BLOOD USING BARBED BEAKS.

POUNCING
PARASITES

Parasites need **no invitation**. These organisms find a **host organism**, attach themselves to it, and **reap all the benefits**.

Tongue-tied
Inside the mouth of this pink anemonefish is a tongue-eating louse parasite. *Cymothoa exigua* enters through the fish's gills, latches onto its tongue, and settles in for a feast.

LEUCOCHLORIDIUM PARADOXUM DISRUPTS A SNAIL'S INSTINCT TO AVOID DAYLIGHT, MAKING IT VULNERABLE.

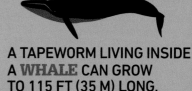

A TAPEWORM LIVING INSIDE A WHALE CAN GROW TO 115 FT (35 M) LONG.

The frog and the flatworm
Parasitic flatworms give tadpoles a terrible time, forcing themselves into the tissue that will later become the frog's legs. The adult frog ends up with deformed, missing, or extra limbs.

Shell shock
The *Leucochloridium paradoxum* flatworm infests the digestive systems of birds and passes to snails feeding on bird droppings. The parasite moves to the snail's tentacles where it is mistaken for caterpillars by hungry birds, and the cycle continues.

Hatching a plan
The female sabre wasp lays its eggs on the larvae of the wood wasp using its large ovipositor to drill into infested wood. When the eggs hatch into larvae, they eat their hosts alive.

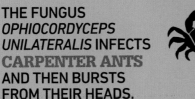

THE FUNGUS *OPHIOCORDYCEPS UNILATERALIS* INFECTS CARPENTER ANTS AND THEN BURSTS FROM THEIR HEADS.

THE PARASITE *SACCULINA CARCINI* INVADES CRABS, SPREADING LIKE TENDRILS INSIDE THEIR BODIES.

PARASITE FOR
SORE EYES

Blink and you'll miss them, but **minuscule parasites** have taken up residence on your **eyelashes**. Here, they've found a comfortable home and an **endless food supply** without even an invite. And the older you get, the more mites come to stay!

Each eyelash mite is just 0.3 mm long—difficult to see with the naked eye.

Though eyelashes are the preferred location, these mites will also infest the nose, cheeks, and forehead.

WHILE PEOPLE SLEEP, EYELASH MITES EMERGE FROM THE HAIR FOLLICLES TO MATE AND THEN RETURN TO LAY EGGS.

EYELASH MITES ARE TRANSFERRED FROM PERSON TO PERSON BY PHYSICAL CONTACT.

FAST FACTS

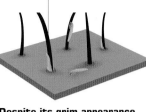

Several mites occupy each hair follicle.

Despite its grim appearance, this wormlike mite is harmless. Some scientists claim eyelash mites actually do good because they keep follicles clean. The mites spend most of their time face down in hair follicles, clearing harmful dirt.

Eyelash mites, *Demodex folliculorum* and *Demodex brevis*, are skin scavengers that bury themselves face down in hair follicles to feast on the dead cells and oily secretions. Older people have oilier skin and weaker immune systems, so greater numbers of mites congregate on their eyelashes.

SKIN STALKERS

Another uninvited guest is the dust mite. Visible as tiny specks of dust, these mites thrive on dead skin flakes, which constantly fall off people. These troublemakers are a common cause of sneezes and asthma.

BABIES ARE BORN WITH NO PARASITES, BUT IMPURITIES BUILD UP ON THE SKIN OVER TIME.

0.05

A HUMAN SHEDS **0.05 OZ (1.5 G)** OF SKIN EVERY DAY— ENOUGH TO FEED A MILLION DUST MITES.

This caterpillar is the larval stage of the *Hemeroplanes triptolemus* moth.

SNAKE IN
THE GRASS

When is a snake not a snake? When it's a **caterpillar**! This extraordinary disguise is **self-defense**. The snake mimic hawkmoth caterpillar does an **uncanny impression** of a scary snake to avoid its forest predators.

CATERPILLARS OF THE GIANT PEACOCK MOTH DETER PREDATORS BY CHIRPING ULTRASONIC SOUNDS.

CATERPILLARS OF THE MOTH *NEMORIA ARIZONARIA* MIMIC A CATKIN (HANGING FLOWER CLUSTER).

The brown area that forms the top of the "head" is actually the caterpillar's underside—its legs are visible if you look closely.

CAMOUFLAGE CATERPILLARS

Caterpillars use every trick in the book to deter an attack. Some resemble unappealing bird droppings (above), while others have false "eyespots" to make themselves appear more threatening. Other species develop prickly spines and hairy clumps to look less appetizing to predators.

FAST FACTS

Clinging to a branch, the snake mimic hawkmoth caterpillar looks very ordinary.

If something alarms the caterpillar, it throws itself backward, twisting its body to show its underside.

The caterpillar then inflates the head-end of its body to create a realistic-looking snake's head.

The caterpillar pulls in its head and expands the front part of its body to form a realistic snake's head.

If this hawkmoth caterpillar feels threatened, it immediately takes on snakelike characteristics and behavior. Pulling in its legs and head, the caterpillar adopts a slithering motion. Its underside grows larger, giving the semblance of a snake's head. The body is large by caterpillar standards and covered in scales, ensuring this species is one convincing masquerader.

PUSS MOTH CATERPILLARS PUFF UP AND SQUIRT HARMFUL ACID TO SCARE AWAY PREDATORS.

LOBSTER MOTH CATERPILLARS MIMIC AN ANT AT THE FRONT AND A SCORPION OR LOBSTER AT THE BACK.

FLYING
FIGURES

Considered a **sign of good fortune** in their native Central and South America, these butterflies have markings that look like numbers— **88 and 89**. Emblazoned across each wing, the **striking digits** help this species **attract mates** amidst the flora and fauna.

These high-speed fliers travel solo through their tropical rainforest homes.

WINDOW WINGS

You can see right through the Glasswing butterfly. Its transparent wings resemble panes of glass, helping the species evade predators in its Central and South American domain.

 A **BUTTERFLY'S SCALES** ARE NO MORE THAN 0.1 MM IN LENGTH.

 SOME BUTTERFLIES WITH IRIDESCENT WINGS HAVE A **JEWEL-LIKE** APPEARANCE.

These **butterflies land on people** in summer to **sup on their sweat**.

FAST FACTS

Tiny scales scatter the light, creating beautiful iridescent colors.

Butterfly wings are covered with thousands of tiny scales made from a substance called chitin. These scales give the insects their striking colors as well as help regulate their body temperature.

The numerals **89** or **88** appear clearly on the underside of each wing.

The exact markings of these butterflies (*Diaethria sp.*) depend on the specific subspecies. There are 12 species, with the markings taking a different form, color, and shape each time. Sadly, their number is dwindling—they are often killed for their exotic wings, which are used in the production of tourist souvenirs.

OWL BUTTERFLIES OF CENTRAL AND SOUTH AMERICA HAVE EYELIKE SPOTS TO SCARE PREDATORS.

11 WITH A WINGSPAN OF ABOUT 11 IN (27 CM), THE FEMALE QUEEN ALEXANDRA'S BIRDWING IS THE WORLD'S LARGEST BUTTERFLY.

DEVIL IN
DISGUISE

Is it a leaf? Is it tree bark? No, it's the **satanic leaf-tailed gecko**. Cleverly disguised as a rotting leaf, Madagascar's **camouflage king** has red eyes and a taste for night hunting—it's nature's most **devilish deceiver**.

FAST FACTS

Many geckos have sticky toe pads that allow them to cling to various surfaces. Each toe is ridged and covered in thousands of tiny bristles, which are divided into billions of microscopic hairs. These hairs lock with irregularities in the surface the gecko is climbing, giving it grip.

Ridged toes

Stalklike bristles

Minuscule hairs

Leaf-tailed geckos have no eyelids but use their long tongues to wipe away dust.

THIS GECKO HAS A BRIGHT RED MOUTH, WHICH IS REVEALED WHEN IT PRODUCES A LOUD SCREAM.

SOME GECKOS HAVE STICKY PADS ON THEIR TAIL TIPS TO HELP CLIMB TREES.

This mini-monster epitomizes survival of the fittest, having adapted gradually to become today's extraordinary leaf impersonator. Snakes and rats target the gecko—if the disguise fails, the brave battler falls to the forest floor, hoping to disappear in the foliage, or leaps to a higher branch for shelter.

MOSSY MASK

Madagascar's mossy leaf-tailed gecko is another master of disguise. Its color and markings make it look exactly like mossy tree bark. A fringe of skin flattens the gecko against the tree so that, when still, it blends seamlessly into its forest habitat.

The twisted body and veiny skin echo the detail of a dry leaf, which ensures the gecko blends in with its forest home.

The mottled tail appears to have sections missing, as though it has withered over time.

GECKOS STICK TO ANYTHING, EXCEPT **NONSTICK PANS**, WHICH ARE COATED WITH A MATERIAL CALLED TEFLON.

THE SCIENCE BEHIND GECKO FEET IS BEING USED TO DESIGN **ROBOTS** THAT CAN "STICK" TO SPACECRAFT.

IN
HIDING

Standing out from the crowd leaves you **vulnerable** in the **animal kingdom**. Where conflicts are fierce, food is scarce, and lives are on the line, **blending in** can be the best bet for **survival**.

Sly fox
As snowy white as its tundra home, the Arctic fox blends in easily with the icy winter surroundings. But this colored coat changes with the seasons—summer sees the fox sport a reddish brown fur better suited to the bare rock and plants.

Tree mimic
The African scops owl uses its camouflaged plumage and twiglike ear tufts to conceal itself, then swoops suddenly on insects and rodents.

WITH ITS PERFECT TWIGLIKE BODY, THIS STICK INSECT IS A MASTER OF DISGUISE! IT IS ALSO THE LONGEST INSECT ON EARTH.

TIGERS HAVE A STRIPED COAT THAT ENABLES THEM TO BLEND IN WITH THE VEGETATION AND AMBUSH PREY.

Secretive spider
Europe's green huntsman spider is the perfect shade to merge with nearby foliage. The arachnid can move virtually unseen by both predators and prey.

Armed attacker
This vivid inhabitant of Australia's Great Barrier Reef resembles part of the coral but is actually a stonefish. With toxic spines ready, it waits to ambush passing prey.

Adaptable amphibian
The African red toad spends its days hiding under logs or on dead leaves, using its colors and patterned skin to keep safe, while nights are spent searching out insects.

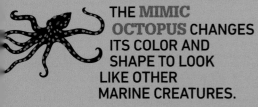

THE **MIMIC OCTOPUS** CHANGES ITS COLOR AND SHAPE TO LOOK LIKE OTHER MARINE CREATURES.

THE **GREEN TREE PYTHON** BLENDS IN PERFECTLY WITH ITS TREETOP HIDEOUT.

GOAT
GYMNASTS

No kidding—the **goats of Tamri village** in Morocco show great agility in **searching for their favorite food**. These nimble nibblers claw, jump, and scramble up **argan trees** to reach their beloved berries, setting in motion a **practice** that's been around for centuries.

INTREPID IBEX

In 2010, a herd of Alpine ibex walked across the nearly vertical face of Italy's Cingino Dam. Despite the 164 ft (50 m) drop beneath them, the agile ibex searched for a snack—salt and lichen between the dam's stones.

Argan berries are a good source of income in this otherwise barren land. Goats gorge on them and pass the hard nuts in their droppings. Locals collect the poop before removing and washing the nuts. These are ground and pressed to make expensive argan oil, used in salad dressings and cosmetic treatments.

IBEX CAN **LEAP** 6 FT (1.8 M), WHICH HELPS THEM CLIMB MOUNTAINOUS TERRAIN WITH EASE.

WESTERN FENCE LIZARDS DO **PUSH-UPS** TO SHOW THAT THEY ARE STRONG AND FIT.

The olivelike argan berry is perfect nourishment in an area where food is scarce.

The **Tamri goats can** climb 30 ft (9 m) up to the **treetops**.

Goats are curious by nature, reveling in opportunities to climb and explore.

FAST FACTS

Goats are good climbers because of their cloven hoofs. The two sides push apart to grip a surface. The hoof has a soft inner part that aids grip, while the animal's dewclaws help provide stability.

Dewclaws

Hard outer hoof

Hoof is cloven (split into two)

Soft inner part

ANTS CAN LIFT OBJECTS THAT WEIGH UP TO **20 TIMES** THEIR BODY WEIGHT.

160

FLYING SQUIRRELS CAN GLIDE FOR MORE THAN 160 FT (50 M) BEFORE LANDING.

DANCE
FEVER

The lord of the dance on the island of Madagascar is the **Verreaux's sifaka**. Fancy footwork has made this **species of lemur** a global sensation, but these moves have real purpose. **Whirling and twirling** through the forest helps them **evade predators**.

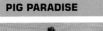

Sifakas have splayed feet, which make it difficult to walk. Instead, they "dance"—hopping sideways rapidly on their back legs.

PIG PARADISE

Pigs can't fly, but they can swim! A family of wild porkers enjoys an idyllic island lifestyle on Big Major Cay in the Bahamas. They take daily dips, heading for boats in case people drop food. Sailors are said to have left the pigs on the island, intending to return for a bacon bonanza, but they never did.

Verreaux's sifakas are named after their distinctive noisy cry that sounds like "shif-auk!"

FEMALE VERREAUX'S SIFAKAS CAN LEAP WITH BABIES ON THEIR CHESTS OR BACKS.

VERREAUX'S SIFAKAS LOVE SUNBATHING, ESPECIALLY SUNNING THEIR TUMMIES WHER THEY HAVE LESS HAIR.

The sifaka holds its arms up near its head for balance, while its springy step means it can escape fast, should a predator attack.

As dawn breaks, groups of **Verreaux's sifakas** perform a dazzling dance display. They swing, leap, and bound their way to the feeding grounds where they forage for food. Only in the safety of the treetops can they sit back to munch on a variety of plants unique to the African island.

FAST FACTS

Sifakas are not only nimble on the ground. They also use their powerful hind legs and upright position to leap from tree to tree, often clearing distances of more than 30 ft (9 m).

MEASURING ONLY 4 IN (10 CM), MADAME BERTHE'S MOUSE LEMUR IS THE SMALLEST PRIMATE IN THE WORLD.

SPRINGBOKS PRONK—AN AFRIKAANS WORD FOR "SHOW OFF." THEY LEAP HIGH INTO THE AIR IF THREATENED.

IN-FLIGHT
FIGHT

At first glance, **fur and feathers** appear to have forged an **incredible friendship** in this photograph. A weasel **hitches a ride** on a woodpecker's back as they soar the skies together. In reality, this picture catches on camera the **ultimate airborne animal attack**.

A **sign** now marks the spot where the sensational snap was taken.

ANIMAL ALLIANCES

The animal kingdom can be about forming friendships rather than fighting foes. In Ireland, a dog named Ben and a dolphin named Duggie enjoy chummy swims together, while best friends Fum the cat and Gebra the owl were viewed playing together by one million people on YouTube.

THE NOCTULE BAT HUNTS IN THE AIR, CATCHING SONGBIRDS IN MIDFLIGHT.

LEOPARD SEALS WAIT AT THE EDGE OF THE ICE TO AMBUSH PENGUINS.

In 2015, amateur photographer Martin **LeMay** shot this image in Hornchurch Country Park, London, but the picture doesn't tell the full story. The weasel attacked the woodpecker and refused to give up, even when the bird took flight. An aerial scrap ensued before the weasel tumbled and the woodpecker escaped.

FAST FACTS

The least weasel's body is just bigger than a man's hand.

The tail can be up to 3.1 in (8 cm) long.

The least weasel is the world's smallest carnivore. Measuring only 4.3–10.2 in (11–26 cm) and weighing as little as 0.9 oz (25 g), it has been known to kill prey much bigger than its own size. It is found throughout North America, Europe, and parts of Asia.

The carnivorous least weasel typically attacks large prey, such as rabbits, mice, frogs, and birds.

The European green woodpecker often leaves itself vulnerable to attack because it forages on the ground for ants.

HARPY EAGLES CAN FLY OFF WITH SLOTHS AND MONKEYS WEIGHING UP TO 40 LB (18 KG).

OWEN THE HIPPO AND MZEE THE GIANT TORTOISE BECAME FRIENDS AFTER THE 2004 TSUNAMI.

DEDICATED
DAD

Assumptions about the **female of the species** giving birth are true of most creatures, but **reproduction** is **all at sea** for seahorses. It's **the male** of this odd-looking fish species that **experiences pregnancy and childbirth**, to sighs of relief from female seahorses everywhere!

The young seahorses, or fry, emerge from the opening in the brood pouch.

Muscular contractions expel the young seahorses from the pouch.

SHARK SPAWN

The frilled shark has the longest gestation period of any vertebrate species. Like seahorses, they are ovoviviparous—their young hatch from eggs inside the parent's body. Embryos then grow inside the mother for a staggering three and a half years before finally being born.

This male seahorse's pouch is full of fry.

SPOTTED SEAHORSES MATE WITH JUST ONE PARTNER FOR LIFE.

MALE SPOTTED SEAHORSES USUALLY GIVE BIRTH AT NIGHT DURING A FULL MOON.

The female seahorse makes the eggs inside her body. Male and female entwine tails and perform a long courtship dance that ends with the female depositing the eggs in the male's pouch. The male fertilizes the eggs, and they hatch inside his pouch. The embryos take in everything they need, from oxygen to food, in a gestation period that lasts up to four weeks.

Fewer than five in 1,000 young seahorses survive into adulthood.

FAST FACTS

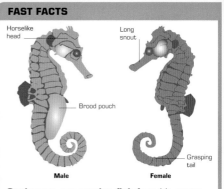

Horselike head

Long snout

Brood pouch

Grasping tail

Male

Female

Seahorses are marine fish found in warm, shallow waters all over the world. Their bodies are protected by bony plates, rather than scales. Poor swimmers, they use their grasping tail to cling to vegetation and their long snout to suck up plankton.

0.25 A SPOTTED SEAHORSE MEASURES ONLY **0.25 IN** (6 MM) IN LENGTH AT BIRTH.

UNLIKE MOST OTHER FISH, SEAHORSES HAVE **EYES** THAT ROTATE IN THEIR SOCKETS.

SHOAL-
STOPPER

Millions of sardines cause an **amazing annual spectacle** by swimming in one **supersize shoal** along South Africa's eastern coastline, to the delight of hungry ocean predators. The **sardine run** is plagued with danger, and the reason for this **mega migration** is unknown.

MARINE MIGRATION

From small sardines to whopper whales, all kinds of marine life migrate. Humpback whales travel from their breeding areas near the equator to the food-rich waters of the Arctic and Antarctica in the summer, covering a distance of up to 5,095 miles (8,200 km).

A sardine baitball is 33–66 ft (10–20 m) in diameter.

A SARDINE SHOAL CONSISTS OF ABOUT 10 MILLION FISH.

A SHOAL OFTEN EXTENDS TO A DEPTH OF 98 FT (30 M).

Under threat, the sardines squash up into a neat baitball so that no individual fish can be singled out.

FAST FACTS

The migrating sardines travel north along the east coast of South Africa, from their spawning ground of Agulhas Bank to the subtropical waters off the coast of Durban. The huge shoals can be 9.3 miles (15 km) long.

Sardines are an integral part of the ocean food chain, with their sheer quantity sustaining many other fish species.

As the tiny fish make their journey, predators gather for a feeding frenzy. Dolphins round up the sardines into baitballs, while birds descend from the skies and sharks converge in the water. The risky migration's motive is unclear, but it may be that the southern waters become too cold for the sardines.

THE BIGGEST SARDINE SHOALS ARE OFTEN **VISIBLE FROM SPACE.**

WITH PREDATORS ON THE PROWL, A BAITBALL USUALLY LASTS ONLY **10–20 MINUTES.**

MURKY
MONSTERS

A **monster's ball** is underway in the deep ocean. You'll want to keep your head above water once you see these **bizarre beasts** of the **seabed**.

Confident cucumber
The transparent sea cucumber shows everything off, including its digestive system! Formally known as *Enypniastes*, it feeds on sediment and moves around on its tentacles.

SEA CUCUMBERS RELEASE THEIR INTERNAL ORGANS TO ENTANGLE PREDATORS AND THEN GROW NEW ORGANS.

NO BIGGER THAN THE SIZE OF A PENCIL, DRAGONFISH SWALLOW PREY HALF THEIR SIZE.

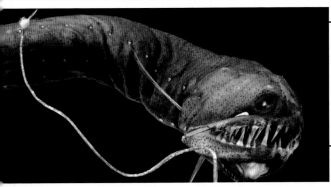

Jawdropper
The scaleless deep-sea dragonfish is a scary sight. With oversize jaws and razor-sharp teeth, this predatory fish produces a light to lure smaller fish and crustaceans to their deaths.

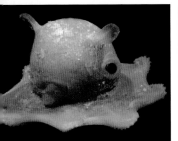

Squashed octopus
Despite its name, the flapjack octopus is not remotely appetizing! The name comes from its compressed bottom, which makes this species appear flatter than other octopuses.

Fearsome fangs
Nicknamed "ogrefish" for its off-putting appearance, *Anoplogaster cornuta* has a tough, bony body. Commonly known as the fangtooth, it is the fish with the biggest teeth in relation to its body size.

A **FLAPJACK OCTOPUS** WEIGHS THE SAME AS A SLICE OF BREAD.

THE **FANGTOOTH** GRABS ITS PREY WITH ITS DAGGERLIKE TEETH BEFORE SWALLOWING IT WHOLE.

Forces of nature

When nature is unleashed in all its glory, the results are spectacular. Super storms tear the skies apart, vast dust clouds leave chaos in their wake, and fiery tornadoes cause carnage on the ground. Nature's mysteries also remind us of its all-pervading power— from stones that seem to sail across the desert to strange sand structures sculpted by lightning.

A fire rainbow, or circumhorizontal arc, forms in high-altitude wispy summer clouds where plate-shaped ice crystals are present. The sun's rays must penetrate the ice crystals at an exact angle for this phenomenon to occur.

WHEN ICE
ATTACKS

Forget the **thunderous roars** of a violent storm: a less dramatic storm produces the most **spectacular** scenes. Known as **ice storms**, they transform the landscape into a **frozen, treacherous world**.

This storm lasted only five minutes, but it was enough to turn cars and trees into ice statues.

STORM DAMAGE

The crust of frozen rain that coats everything after an ice storm can be so thick and heavy that it makes structures like these electricity towers collapse.

ICE DEPOSITS AFTER A STORM CAN MAKE TREE BRANCHES 30 TIMES HEAVIER.

BLACK ICE IS THE INVISIBLE, THIN ICE THAT COVERS ROADS AND PROVES HAZARDOUS TO VEHICLES.

FAST FACTS

Warm air

Cold air

Rain
When frozen precipitation passes through warm air, it melts and falls to the ground as rain.

Freezing rain
If frozen precipitation melts in warm air but cools rapidly as it nears the ground, it freezes on contact.

Sleet
If frozen precipitation thaws in shallow warm air, it refreezes as sleet before it hits the ground.

Snow
When frozen precipitation falls through cold air, it reaches the surface as snow.

Icicles dangling from these tree branches follow the direction of the wind blowing in from Lake Geneva.

Roads and pavements become a treacherous ice rink.

Ice storms are rare events that occur when rain falls through warm air and meets cold air near the ground. The rain freezes on impact, covering everything in a thick, frosty coating. Switzerland's Lake Geneva experienced this ice storm in 2012.

25 AN ICE STORM IN THE US IN 2021 CAUSED MORE THAN **$25 BILLION** OF DAMAGE, MAKING IT THE COSTLIEST WINTER STORM IN US HISTORY.

IN 1998, AN ICE STORM IN CANADA LEFT 3 MILLION PEOPLE **WITHOUT POWER** FOR SIX WEEKS.

SAILING
STONES

Death Valley is the US's **hottest spot**. This remote desert landscape provides a **perfect backdrop** for science-fiction blockbusters such as *Star Wars*, but something stranger than fiction happens here. Heavy rocks **inexplicably move around**. From magnetic fields to alien activity, theories abounded. Finally, we know the truth.

Since the 1900s, scientific research has left no stone unturned. The breakthrough came in 2013, when stones were seen moving on camera. Floating ice proved to be the mischief maker. On cold nights, thin sheets of ice develop, which then melt into smaller pieces during the day, when the sun is shining. Wind pushes the ice along, carrying the rocks with it and depositing them elsewhere.

Early theories suggested that strong winds were responsible for moving the stones. But hurricane-force gusts would be needed to overcome the weight of the heavy rocks.

Each rock travels 7–20 ft (2–6 m) per minute, but in the desert this motion is hard to notice with the naked eye.

1,476

EVEN THE BIGGEST, HEAVIEST STONES HAVE MOVED MORE THAN **1,476 FT** (450 M) FROM THEIR ORIGINAL POSITION.

AS WELL AS MOVING STONES, DUNES IN DEATH VALLEY MOVE TOO, PRODUCING A **HUMMING SOUND** IN THE PROCESS.

FAST FACTS

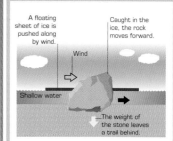

A floating sheet of ice is pushed along by wind.

Caught in the ice, the rock moves forward.

Wind

Shallow water

...The weight of the stone leaves a trail behind.

Rainfall creates a shallow pool in the playa, which then freezes over as the temperature drops. A swift rise in temperature breaks up the ice into smaller, floating sheets. Wind then pushes the ice sheets over the pond. Any rocks caught in the ice sheet are easily carried along by the buoyant ice, inscribing a trail in the mud as they go.

Despite its name, Death Valley is home to more than 400 species of animals.

Racetrack Playa is a dry lake in Death Valley, dotted with large rocks.

STONE COMMANDMENTS

These granite slabs in Elbert County, Georgia, are a mystery set in stone. Known as the Georgia Guidestones, they appeared in 1979 engraved with 10 guidelines for people to follow, which include avoiding useless officials and leaving room for nature. No one knows who wrote the list or who placed these slabs at this location.

THE OLDEST ROCKS IN DEATH VALLEY ARE 1.7 BILLION YEARS OLD BUT LOOK ENTIRELY DIFFERENT TODAY.

135

IN 1913, THE TEMPERATURE IN DEATH VALLEY ROCKETED TO A RECORD-BREAKING **135°F (57°C)**.

WHIPPING UP
A DUST STORM

The incredible **power of nature** is seen when
a violent dust storm blows up, filling the
skies with inescapable banks of **suffocating
cloud**. Tons of whirling sand or soil are
swept along by high winds, leaving
a **trail of devastation** behind.

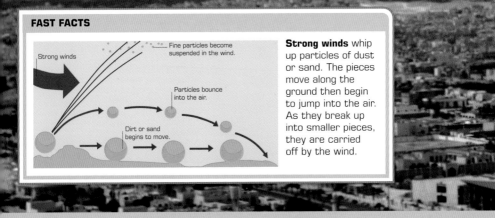

FAST FACTS

Strong winds

Fine particles become
suspended in the wind.

Particles bounce
into the air.

Dirt or sand
begins to move.

Strong winds whip
up particles of dust
or sand. The pieces
move along the
ground then begin
to jump into the air.
As they break up
into smaller pieces,
they are carried
off by the wind.

DUST WHIPPED UP
BY A DUST STORM
CAN REACH 1 MILE
(1.6 KM) IN HEIGHT.

ABOUT 22 MILLION
TONS OF DUST IS
PRESENT IN EARTH'S
ATMOSPHERE AT ANY
GIVEN TIME.

Dust storms are most likely to occur during droughts, when sand or soil is loose and dry. Carried on the wind, billowing dust clouds can envelop entire cities, choking the inhabitants and damaging buildings. This huge dust cloud engulfed the desert city of Riyadh, Saudi Arabia, in March 2009. After the storm passed, parts of the city were left beneath several tons of sand.

DUST DEVILS

Resembling mini tornadoes, dust devils are small-scale whirlwinds, spinning dust in a vertical column of air over the ground. They are less dangerous than their name suggests, usually lasting only a few minutes and rarely causing any damage.

This massive dust storm reduced **visibility** in Riyadh to **zero**.

Flights were grounded at Riyadh's airport as the control tower and runways were blanketed in thick dust.

IN 2010, DROUGHT AND DUST STORMS IN CHINA AFFECTED MORE THAN **15,600 SQ MILES** (40,400 SQ KM) OF LAND.

DUST STORMS ON MARS RESULT IN DUST CLOUDS COVERING CONTINENT-SIZE AREAS FOR WEEKS.

Fulgurite comes from the Latin word for "thunderbolt."

FAST FACTS

The longest fulgurite on record was dug up by researchers from the University of Florida in 1996. This impressive tube had two branches, the longest of which was about 16 ft (5 m) long.

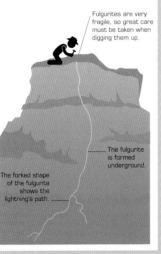

Fulgurites are very fragile, so great care must be taken when digging them up.

The fulgurite is formed underground.

The forked shape of the fulgurite shows the lightning's path.

With its branchlike formation, this sand fulgurite has a rough exterior covered in sand particles, but its interior is smooth and resembles glass.

Sand cools and solidifies quickly after the lightning strike to create the fulgurite. Its size depends on the power of the strike and the depth of the sand.

AN ANCIENT FULGURITE REVEALED THAT **GRASSES AND SHRUBS** GREW IN THE SAHARA DESERT ABOUT 15,000 YEARS AGO.

ON AVERAGE, ABOUT **30 LIGHTNING BOLTS** STRIKE EARTH EVERY SINGLE SECOND.

WHEN LIGHTNING
STRIKES

No matter how long you keep staring and guessing, these **oddball objects** are almost impossible to fathom. Called **fulgurites**, they are the **remarkable and rare** result of what can happen when lightning strikes planet Earth.

A fulgurite is formed when a lightning bolt with a minimum temperature of 3,270°F (1,800°C) strikes sand or rock. Heat melts the substance on impact, fusing the grains into natural glass tubes that follow the branching structure of the lightning bolt deep underground. Over time, the sand around the fulgurite shifts, exposing the fragile tube. Most fulgurites are made from sand, reflected in the unusually high number in the Sahara Desert.

ETERNAL STORM

There is never any calm before the storm at Venezuela's Catatumbo River. Thanks to a unique bank of storm clouds, an "everlasting storm" rages here, producing 1.2 million lightning strikes a year. Known as Catatumbo lightning, this incredible light show is visible 250 miles (400 km) away.

ABOUT 150 CASES OF LIGHTNING CAUSED BY ERUPTING VOLCANOES HAVE BEEN RECORDED OVER 200 YEARS.

TEN MINUTES OF CATATUMBO LIGHTNING COULD LIGHT UP ALL OF SOUTH AMERICA.

SUPER
STORMS

Most thunderstorms develop from **updrafts of rising air**, with the most violent and speedy ones called **supercells**. These long-lasting storms are rare but deadly—they can **unleash havoc** in the form of whirling tornadoes, giant hailstones, punishing winds, and flash floods. Take cover!

Earth experiences about 45,000 thunderstorms a day, but only a few of these are supercells, the worst of all storms. Created by rapidly rotating updrafts of warm, moist air, these super storms carry huge amounts of water and bring extreme weather. The top of the thunderclouds can reach as high as 10 miles (16 km) into the air, while the base may be only 1,640 ft (500 m) above the ground.

Foreboding dark cumulonimbus clouds congregate in the skies before a supercell storm.

A supercell storm often leaves behind considerable damage.

THUNDERCLOUDS CONTAIN UP TO 11,000 TONS OF WATER.

500 A SUPERCELL STORM CAN TRAVEL **500** MILES (800 KM).

FAST FACTS

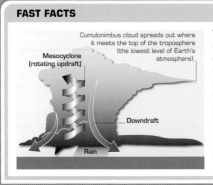

Cumulonimbus cloud spreads out where it meets the top of the troposphere (the lowest level of Earth's atmosphere).

Mesocyclone (rotating updraft)

Downdraft

Rain

Thunderstorms are formed by warm updrafts rising to create cumulonimbus clouds. Cold rain drags air down, creating a cold downdraft. When there is more downdraft than updraft, the storm fizzles out. In a supercell, the updrafts and downdrafts are in balance, so the storm can keep going for hours. The mesocyclone (rapidly rotating updraft) at the storm's core carries huge amounts of water upward so the cloud grows bigger and bigger.

Lightning is about 54,000°F (30,000°C)— hotter than the surface of the sun.

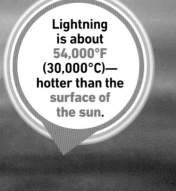

BALL LIGHTNING

During a supercell storm, other odd things can happen. Luminous, ball-shaped objects have appeared a few yards above the ground, bouncing around in a random pattern. Scientists can't agree on the reason for this phenomenon, known as ball lightning.

LIGHTNING CAN STRIKE AS FAR AWAY AS 15 MILES (25 KM) FROM A THUNDERSTORM.

IN JAPAN, GODS REPRESENT THE FORCES OF NATURE— THE GOD OF THUNDER IS A STRONG MAN BEATING DRUMS.

WEIRD
WEATHER

Extreme weather can be **challenging** for meteorologists to predict, and the consequences are often **devastating**.

Twisting tornado
More than 1,200 tornadoes rip across the US every year, with wind speeds crossing 200 mph (320 km/h) and leaving trails of devastation behind them. Canada has the second-highest number—this one is twisting across Elie, Manitoba.

Destructive Katrina
When Hurricane Katrina tore across southeastern US in 2005, it became the country's costliest natural disaster. Winds raged at 175 mph (280 km/h), leaving entire neighborhoods in ruins.

161 THE TRAIL OF DEVASTATION LEFT BY HURRICANE KATRINA COST **$161 BILLION**.

A TORNADO'S **SPINNING WINDS** CAN UPROOT TREES AND LIFT CARS AND BUILDINGS OVER LONG DISTANCES.

Wild waves
Triggered by a huge offshore earthquake, the Indian Ocean tsunami on December 26, 2004, occurred without warning and heaped havoc on southern Asia. Giant waves devastated coastal communities and killed more than 200,000 people, displacing thousands more.

Heavy hail
In 2003 a thunderstorm near Moses, New Mexico, produced hailstones the size of golf balls. Huge hail can easily smash car windshields and injure people on the ground.

Deadly shower
All sorts of things have fallen from the skies, including frogs, bats, fish, insects, jellyfish, and worms. Strong winds can take creatures from shallow ponds and carry them until they fall back down to Earth. In 2010, thousands of dead birds mysteriously rained over Arkansas.

A **TSUNAMI** TRAVELS AS FAST AS A JET PLANE IN THE OPEN OCEAN BUT SLOWS DOWN TO THE SPEED OF A CAR WHEN THE WAVES HIT THE SHORE.

A **GIANT HAILSTONE** CAN BE UP TO 8 IN (20 CM) WIDE AND WEIGH 2 LB (1 KG).

BUBBLING
UNDER

On the surface, **Lake Abraham** in the **Canadian Rocky Mountains** is a photographer's dream. But beneath the frozen waters lie **towers of bubbles**, suspended in ice. These beautiful bubbles hide an ugly secret—they contain **harmful methane gas**.

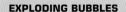

EXPLODING BUBBLES

Methane is a colorless, odorless gas, but it is highly flammable. Scientists studying the frozen bubbles (above) may be unsure which gas they've found. Piercing the ice with a pick and igniting the gas produces explosive results—and proves the gas is methane.

METHANE **BUBBLES** PILE UP ON LAKE ABRAHAM, AS IF A BUBBLE-MAKING MACHINE STOPPED IN MIDFLOW.

25 METHANE GAS IS **25 TIMES** BETTER AT TRAPPING HEAT IN EARTH'S ATMOSPHERE THAN CARBON DIOXIDE.

Lake Abraham is an artificial lake, created in 1972 by damming the North Saskatchewan River.

Methane gas forms in thousands of lakes. Lake Abraham has high levels because it was created by flooding a valley, so there is a lot of plant matter on the lake bed.

Lake Abraham's methane bubbles are produced by bacteria on the lake bed feeding on dead plant matter. In the summer, the gas rises to the surface and escapes, but when the lake freezes over, the bubbles are trapped in the ice. Methane is a greenhouse gas, which traps heat in the atmosphere and contributes to global warming.

FAST FACTS

Earth's atmosphere allows the sun's heat to reach Earth and stops some from escaping. This is known as the greenhouse effect, and it warms Earth enough to support life. Increasing levels of methane and other greenhouse gases are contributing to the "enhanced greenhouse effect" by trapping more heat and causing Earth's temperature to rise.

Heat from the sun passes through the atmosphere and warms Earth.

Some of the heat escapes into space.

Greenhouse gases trap some of the heat in the atmosphere.

EVERY YEAR COWS ON EARTH PRODUCE ENOUGH METHANE TO FILL **40 MILLION** HOT AIR BALLOONS.

A GLOBAL TEMPERATURE INCREASE OF **35.6°F (2°C)** WOULD KILL 99% OF CORALS.

LIGHT
SHOW

When Earth's **magnetic field** is disturbed by the sun's solar wind, the night sky lights up with **dancing streaks of color**. While the Northern lights (Aurora Borealis) usually steal the show, **the Southern lights** (Aurora Australis) are equally impressive but less accessible.

PLANETARY AURORAS

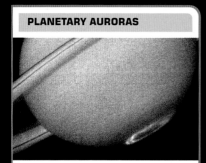

Intrepid explorers can spot auroras in space. Giant Jupiter has a strong magnetic field that reacts with its moons, producing vibrant lights. Saturn has auroras at the north and south poles. Similar sights have been seen on Uranus, Neptune, and Mars.

This dazzling display of Aurora Australis over Antarctica is seen from space. ⋯⋯⋯⋯

Antarctica is surrounded by open water, so there is limited opportunity for people to find a viewing platform from which to enjoy the Aurora Australis. ⋯⋯⋯⋯

AN AURORA WAS FIRST DESCRIBED ON A **BABYLONIAN CLAY TABLET** IN 567 BCE.

AURORAS CAN STRETCH FOR **190 MILES** (300 KM) INTO THE ATMOSPHERE.

Auroras occur when the solar wind—electrically charged particles escaping the sun—becomes trapped by Earth's magnetic field. The particles are funneled toward Earth's two poles, colliding with gases in the atmosphere. These collisions produce Aurora Borealis at the north magnetic pole, around the Arctic Circle, and Aurora Australis at the south magnetic pole, around the Antarctic Circle.

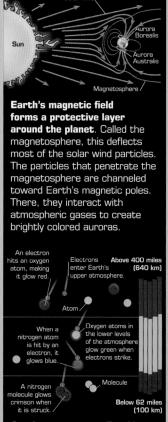

FAST FACTS

Solar wind

Sun

Aurora Borealis

Aurora Australis

Magnetosphere

Earth's magnetic field forms a protective layer around the planet. Called the magnetosphere, this deflects most of the solar wind particles. The particles that penetrate the magnetosphere are channeled toward Earth's magnetic poles. There, they interact with atmospheric gases to create brightly colored auroras.

An electron hits an oxygen atom, making it glow red.

Electrons enter Earth's upper atmosphere.

Above 400 miles (640 km)

Atom

When a nitrogen atom is hit by an electron, it glows blue.

Oxygen atoms in the lower levels of the atmosphere glow green when electrons strike.

A nitrogen molecule glows crimson when it is struck.

Molecule

Below 62 miles (100 km)

As electrons enter Earth's upper atmosphere, they meet atoms of oxygen and nitrogen at altitudes high above Earth's surface. The color of the aurora depends on which atom is struck, and the altitude of the meeting.

In the past, auroras were considered a premonition of war or plague.

AURORAS PRODUCE HISSING OR CLAPPING SOUNDS THAT CAN BE HEARD BY HUMANS.

A DISTANT BROWN DWARF STAR HOSTS AURORAS A MILLION TIMES BRIGHTER THAN AURORAS ON EARTH.

SPIKY
SNOW

Resembling an **overgrown garden**, with tall blades of green grass replaced by white snow, penitentes are the **coolest**, **sharpest snow formations** around. It was once wrongly believed that this **pointy Andes snowscape** was carved out by the biting mountain wind.

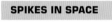

SPIKES IN SPACE

Some scientists think that Jupiter's icy moon Europa is home to penitentes just like those on Earth. These ice blades may stretch up to 33 ft (10 m) tall and could be a nightmare for any future spacecraft attempting to land here.

 PENITENTES ARE NAMED AFTER AN ORDER OF SPANISH MONKS WHO WEAR SPIKY WHITE HATS.

 PENITENTES USUALLY FORM AT HIGH ALTITUDES, IN EXCESS OF 13,000 F (4,000 M).

Let's get straight to the point—wind doesn't create penitentes. These spikes of hardened snow develop where air is cold and dry, allowing the sun to turn snow instantly into water vapor, without melting it first. This is called sublimation. Some areas sublimate quicker, leaving behind towering penitentes.

The height of penitentes ranges from 1 in (3 cm) to a towering 16 ft (5 m).

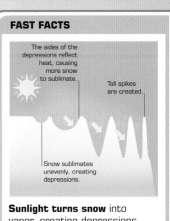

FAST FACTS

The sides of the depressions reflect heat, causing more snow to sublimate.

Tall spikes are created.

Snow sublimates unevenly, creating depressions.

Sunlight turns snow into vapor, creating depressions, which catch more sunlight and so sublimate quicker. The high sides of the depressions become spikes.

English naturalist **Charles Darwin** wrote about **penitentes** in **1839**.

PACKED TOGETHER, THE ICY STRUCTURES OFTEN POINT **TOWARD THE SUN**.

1,600

THE DWARF PLANET PLUTO HAS PENITENTES THAT ARE ABOUT 1,600 FT (488 M) TALL.

ICEBREAKERS

From **giant icebergs** to delicate **frost formations**, ice takes on some strange structures in the world's **coolest places**.

Icy beard
Frost beard resembles silky white hair growing on wood, such as this log in Switzerland. Logs absorb rain, but when the water freezes in cold weather, it expands out onto the wooden exterior, exposing icy "hairs."

Ice stripes
Icebergs are usually white, but this one in Greenland seems to have blue veins! It is an example of striped ice, which occurs when algae, minerals, or sediment in sea water freeze in an iceberg, creating streaks of blue, green, yellow, brown, or black.

FROST BEARD FORMS WHERE THE FUNGUS *EXIDIOPSIS EFFUSA* GROWS ON ROTTING WOOD.

JUST AS WITH SNOWFLAKES, EACH **FROST FLOWER** HAS A UNIQUE PATTERN.

Frost flowers
This pretty but fleeting phenomenon, seen here in the Canadian Rockies, occurs when plants carry water from their roots up into their stems. Ice crystals form, which spread out and split the plant's stem to reveal the frozen "flowers."

Frozen pancakes
Less tasty than normal pancakes but much bigger, ice pancakes develop in colder regions when bits of foam floating on rivers and seas freeze and knock into one another. Circular ice blocks result, enjoyed by these ducks on a river in subzero Belarus.

10 ICE PANCAKES CAN REACH A WHOPPING **10 FT** (3 M) IN WIDTH.

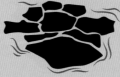

A LIQUID LAYER OF ICE CRYSTALS RESEMBLING AN OIL SPILL IS KNOWN AS **GREASE ICE**.

ALPINE
ALLEY

The **Tateyama Kurobe Alpine Route** is Japan's most spectacular scenic journey. People traveling along the **picturesque passageway** find their view of the **lofty mountains** suddenly obliterated by **towering snow walls** on either side.

> **One million tourists take the Alpine Route each year.**

THE ROUTE IS NICKNAMED "ROOF OF JAPAN" DUE TO ITS HEIGHT OF 7,874 FT (2,400 M).

TOURISTS CAN SEE SNOW KAMAKURAS, JAPANESE IGLOO: ALONG THE ROUT

Diggers clear heavy snow to produce the 65 ft (20 m) high snow corridor every spring, which stretches for 1,640 ft (500 m).

SNOW TUNNELS

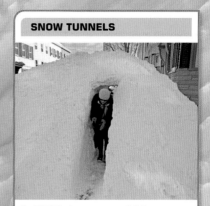

In 2015, heavy snowfall in North America resulted in locals digging their own snow tunnels to get out and about. Teams of diggers also constructed a variety of tunnels ranging in depth and length to help commuters and cyclists keep on the move.

FAST FACTS

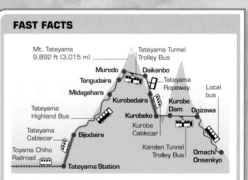

Mt. Tateyama
9,892 ft (3,015 m)

Tateyama Tunnel
Trolley Bus

Murodo   Daikanbo
Tengudaira   Tateyama
Midagahara   Ropeway
Kurobedaira   Kurobe   Local
Tateyama   Dam   bus
Highland Bus   Kurobeko   Ogizawa
Tateyama   Kurobe
Cablecar   Bijodaira   Cablecar
Toyama Chiho   Kanden Tunnel
Railroad   Trolley Bus   Omachi
Tateyama Station   Onsenkyo

The terrain is tricky on many parts of the 56-mile (90 km) long Tateyama Kurobe Alpine Route, so a number of different modes of transportation are used along the way, including trolley buses, cable cars, and ropeways.

This panoramic route opened in 1971 and is open each year from April to November. It is best known for the staggeringly high snow walls of Murodo, which in some years are as tall as a 10-story building. Other landmark sites along the route include the Kurobe Dam and Hida Mountains.

THE NEARBY VILLAGE OF SHIRAKAWA-GO HAS HOUSES WITH UNIQUE JAPANESE-STYLE **THATCHED ROOFS**.

A SEPARATE **PANORAMA ROAD** PROVIDES A VIEW OF MOUNT TSURUGI, ONE OF THE TALLEST PEAKS IN THE HIDA MOUNTAINS.

MORNING
GLORY

Like a magical highway running straight through the sky, **morning glory clouds** are an **extraordinary weather phenomenon**. A rarity in the rest of the world, they roll around regularly in **remote regions** of northern Australia, caused by wavelike currents in the air.

BUBBLING SKIES

When the sky appears to be covered in bubble wrap, it's most likely mammatus clouds. Usually associated with bad weather, these harmless clouds appear as a collection of droopy bulges underneath storm clouds.

MORNING GLORY CLOUDS ARE 1 MILE (2 KM) WIDE AND 0.6 MILES (1 KM) DEEP.

CLOUDS SHAPED LIKE OCEAN WAVES ARE CALLED KELVIN–HELMHOLTZ CLOUDS.

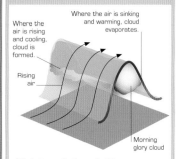

FAST FACTS

Where the air is rising and cooling, cloud is formed.

Where the air is sinking and warming, cloud evaporates.

Rising air

Morning glory cloud

These mysterious banks of clouds stretch across the sky from one horizon to the other. Appearing regularly in early morning between September and November, the clouds form in northeastern Australia's Gulf of Carpentaria, and roll in over Burketown, Queensland. The captivating clouds form on waves in the atmosphere created when moist sea air meets a layer of drier air.

Moisture-laden air blows in from the sea at night, pushing underneath a drier layer of air blown out from the land and creating a wave. The cloud is continuously formed in the upward current of the wave as the moisture-heavy air rises, cools, and condenses. In the downward current, the cloud evaporates. This continuous condensation and evaporation forms the roll-shaped bank of cloud.

Morning glory clouds are a dream come true for hang gliders, who can "surf" them effortlessly, moved by the surrounding thermal winds.

Morning
glory clouds
can be longer
than 600 miles
(1,000 km).

LAYERED LENTICULAR CLOUDS THAT RESEMBLE **UFOS** FORM NEAR MOUNTAINS.

WINTER CLOUDS IN THE POLAR STRATOSPHERE HAVE AN IRIDESCENT SHINE.

SNOW
CHIMNEYS

Winter wonderlands can be home to the unexpected sight of **snow chimneys**, or **fumaroles**, puffing steam into the sky. Occurring in **volcanic regions**, fumaroles are openings in Earth's surface, from which **hot steam** and volcanic gases are emitted.

Gas can be released for centuries or just a few weeks, depending on the heat source.

SNOW ROLLERS

Another unusual eye opener is the snow roller. These giant cylinders develop naturally, as smaller pieces of snow blown by high winds gather more snow in a traditional snowballing effect. They are most commonly seen in cold regions of North America and Europe.

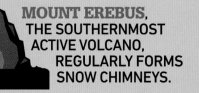

MOUNT EREBUS, THE SOUTHERNMOST ACTIVE VOLCANO, REGULARLY FORMS SNOW CHIMNEYS.

YELLOWSTONE, THE US'S FIRST NATIONAL PARK, IS HOME TO ABOUT 4,000 FUMAROLES.

Close relations of hot springs and gushing geysers, fumaroles require heat and a gas or water source to burst forth. Volcanic magma (molten rock) under Earth's surface provides the heat and gases. When magma comes into contact with groundwater, the water boils and is released as steam.

Carbon dioxide, sulfur dioxide, and hydrogen sulfide are often emitted from a fumarole, and a gas mask should be worn if confronting these dangerous gases.

In Arctic areas, the exiting steam freezes, forming vast snow chimneys around the volcanic opening.

FAST FACTS

These steaming vents in Earth's surface always occur in regions with active volcanism. They work in a similar way to geysers: underground water meets magma and is heated until it boils and bursts through cracks in the rock, making its way to the surface. A fumarole has a smaller reserve of water so emits only steam.

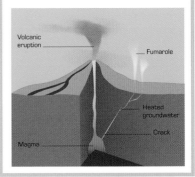

Volcanic eruption

Fumarole

Heated groundwater

Crack

Magma

A **SOLFATARA** IS A SULFUR-RICH FUMAROLE, WHILE A **MOFETTE** IS A FUMAROLE RICH IN CARBON DIOXIDE.

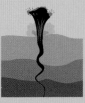

ALTHOUGH MOST **SNOW ROLLERS** ARE TINY, SOME ARE BIGGER THAN A CAR.

IN THE LINE OF
FIRENADOES

Beware **blazing fires** and **whirling winds**. When two of nature's fiercest foes strike at the same time, they create firenadoes (**fire tornadoes**). Twisting flames leap high into the air in a **dangerous spectacle** that can quickly get out of hand.

FIREBALL FRENZY

Science struggles to explain the regular occurrence of fireballs exploding from the Mekong River in Thailand. Locals believe that hundreds of Naga fireballs are released from the mouth of Naga, a legendary snake said to haunt the waters.

This **firenado** started on **burning farmland** in **Chillicothe, Missouri**, in 2014.

A FIRENADO CAN REACH A BLISTERING TEMPERATURE OF **2,000°F (1,093°C)**.

143

THE 2018 CARR FIRE TORNADO IN CALIFORNIA, RAGED AT **SPEEDS** OF 143 MPH (230 KM/H).

If hot air moves rapidly toward cooler air, it can generate a spiraling vortex (whirlwind). This can happen during a storm, causing a tornado. But a fiercely burning fire can create the same effect, with the added element of flames. These firenadoes do not usually last long, but they can be very destructive, hurling burning ashes over a broad area.

Shooting flames can stretch 100 ft (30 m) into the sky.

FAST FACTS

Tornado-like conditions can be created by a raging bush fire. When violent updrafts generated by the fire meet cooler air above, the air starts to spin, forming a funnel.

When the hot updrafts meet cooler air, the air starts to spin.

The intense heat of the bush fire creates violent updrafts.

Oxygen strengthens the flames as the fire is sucked up into the funnel's center, creating a firenado.

Fire and combustible gases are sucked up and fueled by oxygen in the funnel's center. The funnel turns into a jet of flame—a firenado.

 DURING THAILAND'S NAGA FESTIVAL, THOUSANDS OF PEOPLE LINE THE MEKONG TO WATCH THE SPECTACULAR **FIREBALLS** ILLUMINATE THE SKY.

 MANY OF THE GLOWING FIREBALLS THAT RISE FROM THE MEKONG RIVER ARE THE SIZE OF **BASKETBALLS**.

INDEX

ACKNOWLEDGMENTS

The publisher would like to thank the following people for their help with making this book: Arpit Aggarwal, Kathakali Banerjee, Bipasha Basu, Carron Brown, Virien Chopra, Chhavi Nagpal, Rupa Rao, and Fleur Star for editorial assistance; Anastasia Baliyan, Noopur Dalal, Rachael Grady, Spencer Holbrook, Stefan Podhorodecki, Aparajita Sen, Astha Singh, Jemma Westing, and Steve Woosnam-Savage for design assistance; Steve Crozier and Steve Willis for creative retouching; Suhita Dharamjit for the jacket; Claire Gell for jackets coordination on the first edition; Hazel Beynon for proofreading; and Helen Peters for the index.

The publisher would like to thank the following for their kind permission to reproduce their photographs:
(Key: a–above; b–below/bottom; c–center; f–far; l–left; r–right; t–top)

1 Ardea: Thomas Marent 2 Corbis: Paul Williams – Funkystock / imageBROKER (tr). naturepl.com: Visuals Unlimited (br). 3 Alamy Stock Photo: Iain Masterton (tl); Ivan Kuzmin (c). Dreamstime.com: Exposurestonature (bl). National News and Pictures / National News Press Agency: Ken Rotberg Photography (cra). 4–5 Corbis: Paul Williams – Funkystock / imageBROKER (b). 6–7 Tormod Sandtorv. 8 Alamy Stock Photo: age fotostock (bl). 8–9 Corbis: Kazuyoshi Nomachi. 10–11 Getty Images: Mark D Callanan. 11 Alamy Stock Photo: adp-stock (br). Dreamstime.com: Jesús Eloy Ramos Lara (tr). 12 Alamy Stock Photo: All Canada Photos (bl). Dreamstime.com: Microvone (bl). 12–13 Corbis: Gunter Marx Photography. 14 Alamy Stock Photo: National Geographic Image Collection (bl). 14–15 National Geographic Creative: John Stanmeyer. 16–17 123RF.com: derege. 17 Alamy Stock Photo: Sergey Podkolzin (tc). Dreamstime.com: Robert Adrian Hillman (bl). 18–19 Corbis: Imaginechina. 18 Corbis: Viking 1 (bl). 20 Corbis: Michele Falzone / JAI (b). 21 Fotolia: janmiko (bl). Getty Images: Suzanne and Nick Geary (cr). Masterfile: Frank Krahmer (tr). 22–23 Alamy Stock Photo: blickwinkel. 22 NASA: JPL / Space Science Institute (bl). 24–25 Alfred-Wegener-Institute for Polar and Marine Research. 25 Corbis: George Steinmetz (br). 26–27 Corbis: Christophe Boisvieux / Hemis. 27 Corbis: Christophe Boisvieux (br). 28–29 Corbis: Martin Harvey. 28 Dreamstime.com: Artur Kutskyi (bc). 29 FLPA: Chien Lee / Minden Pictures (br). 30 Corbis: Marco Stoppato & Amanda Ronzoni / Visuals Unlimited (bl). 31 Getty Images / iStock: Chikuwabubu (bl). 32–33 Iurie Belegurschi. 33 Corbis: Aaron McCoy / Robert Harding World Imagery (bl). 34–35 Caters News Agency: Mikhail Mishainik (b). 35 Getty Images: Linde Waidehofer / Barcroft Media (cr). Science Photo Library: Javier Trueba / MSF (tr). 36–37 National

Geographic Creative: Stephen Alvarez. 36 Dreamstime.com: Slothastronaut (bl). National Geographic Creative: Stephen Alvarez (bl). 37 Dreamstime.com: Crafteroks (bc). 38–39 FLPA: Gerry Ellis / Minden Pictures. 39 Corbis: Anup Shah (bl). 40–41 AWL Images: Paul Harris. 40 Corbis: Jason Reeve / Demotix (bl). Dreamstime.com: Czarfil1 (bc). 41 Dreamstime.com: Isselee (bl). 42–43 Alamy Stock Photo: Iain Masterton. 44–45 AWL Images: Max Milligan. 44 Dreamstime.com: Andrey Pronin (bl). 45 DK Images: Angela Coppola / University of Pennsylvania Museum of Archaeology and Anthropology (bc). 46–47 Alamy Stock Photo: Paul Springett 10. 46 Rex Features: Imaginechina (bl). 48 Alamy Stock Photo: dpa picture alliance archive (b). Corbis: Wolfgang Rattay / Reuters (cl). 49 Corbis: Wolfgang Rattay / Reuters (br). Getty Images: William West / AFP (tl). TopFoto.co.uk: ullsteinbild (cl). 50–51 Stuart Jackson Carter. 51 Corbis: Marc Dozier (bc). 52 Dreamstime.com: Dreamshot (clb). 52–53 Getty Images: Moment Open. 54 Getty Images: Timothy Allen (bl). 54–55 Frederic Buyle (tr). 56–57 Getty Images: Timothy Allen. 56 Getty Images / iStock: Aisyah az-Zahra (bl). Rex Features: HAP / Quirky China News (bl). 58 Alamy Stock Photo: Pacific Press. 58–59 Dima Chatrov. 60 Alamy Stock Photo: Hemis (bl). 60–61 Corbis: Steve Kaufman. 62 Getty Images: Patrick Aventurier / Gamma-Rapho (bl). 62–63 Alamy Stock Photo: Jim Kidd. 64–65 Alamy Stock Photo: Katya Tsvetkova. 65 Alamy Stock Photo: Danita Delimont (br). 66–67 Google. 66 Google: Street View (bl). 68–69 Getty Images: Stringer / AFP. 68 Dreamstime.com: Macrovector (bl). 69 Alamy Stock Photo: Robert Harding World Imagery (bl). 70–71 Corbis: epa. 70 Getty Images / iStock: DigitalVision Vectors / A-Digit (bc). 71 Corbis: Michael Buholzer / Reuters (tr). 72–73 Alamy Stock Photo: David R. Frazier Photolibrary, Inc.. 72 Alamy Stock Photo: Nancy Hoyt Belcher (bl). 74–75 Corbis: LWA / Larry Williams / Blend Images. 74 Alamy Stock Photo: Jon Arnold Images Ltd (bl). 76–77 Dreamstime.com: Exposurestonature. 78–79 Alamy Stock Photo: Wanda Lotus. 78 Andrea Moro: (bl). 79 Dreamstime.com: Michal Ficel (bc). 80–81 Science Photo Library: Dr Morley Read. 80 Dreamstime.com: Md. Delwar Hossain (bc). laajala/flickr: (bl). 81 Dreamstime.com: Adisorn Sukhamwang (br). 82 Caters News Agency: Eeerkia Schulz (b). 83 Alamy Stock Photo: age fotostock (bl); David Bigwood (cr). NOLEHACE Orchid Photography: (l). 84–85 FLPA: Photo Researchers (b). 85 Corbis: Ch'ien Lee / Minden Pictures (br). FLPA: Photo Researchers (r). 86–87 Rex Features: Amos Chapple. 86 Pooktre / Peter Cook and Becky Northey: (tl). 88–89 SuperStock: Sara Janini / age fotostock. 88 SuperStock: Morales / age fotostock (bl). 90–91 Getty Images: Cultura Travel / Romona Robbins Photography (b). 91 Alamy Stock

Photo: Prisma Bildagentur AG (l); Susan Pease (cr). 92–93 Getty Images / iStock: crbellette. 92 Alamy Stock Photo: Ecoimage (bl). Dreamstime.com: Vera Kudareva (bl). 94–95 Alamy Stock Photo: epa european pressphoto agency b.v. 95 Getty Images: Lam Yik Fei (bc). 96–97 Corbis: Taylor Lockwood / Visuals Unlimited. 97 biologyforums.com: (bl). 98 Alamy Stock Photo: imageBROKER (bl). Corbis: Josef Beck / imageBROKER (cr). 99 Alamy Stock Photo: Arco Images GmbH (cl). Corbis: Ch'ien Lee / Minden Pictures (r). 100–101 Corbis: Doug Perrine / Nature Picture Library. 101 Science Photo Library: Brian Brake (crb). 102 Alamy Stock Photo: Marvin Dembinsky Photo Associates (bl). 102–103 Alamy Stock Photo: Ivan Kuzmin. 104 Corbis: Michael Durham / Minden Pictures (bl). 104–105 Caters News Agency: Gary Tindale. 106–107 Caters News Agency: Antero Topp. 107 Photoshot: NHPA (br). 108 Alamy Stock Photo: Ethan Daniels (b). 109 Corbis: Juan Medina / Reuters (tl); Michael Edwards / Great Stock (br). Rex Features: Mint Images (cl). 110–111 Alamy Stock Photo: Richard Ellis. 110 Alamy Stock Photo: Marvin Dembinsky Photo Associates (cl). 112–113 Corbis: Department for International Development / Russell Watkins. 113 Corbis: Stephen Frink (br). 114–115 Jurgen Otto. 115 Corbis: Tim Laman / National Geographic Creative (br). 116 Corbis: Dr. David Phillips / Visuals Unlimited (br). 116–117 Science Photo Library: Eye Of Science. 117 Science Photo Library: Eye Of Science (br). 118 Alamy Stock Photo: Ethan Daniels (b). 119 Alamy Stock Photo: Frank Hecker (cl); Michael Doolittle (tr). FLPA: Gianpiero Ferrari (br). 120–121 Science Photo Library: Eye Of Science. 121 Alamy Stock Photo: Science Photo Library (br). 122–123 Science Photo Library: Dr George Beccaloni. 123 Richard Seaman: (tr). 124 Corbis: Michael Weber / imageBROKER (bl). 124–125 naturepl.com: Visuals Unlimited. 125 Getty Images: Visuals Unlimited, Inc. / Thomas Marent. Getty Images / iStock: ekolara (bl). 126–127 Ardea: Thomas Marent. 127 Alamy Stock Photo: Scott Buckel (tr). 128–129 FLPA: Matthias Breiter / Minden Pictures (b). 128 Dreamstime.com: VetraKori (bl). Getty Images: Gallo Images (cl). 129 Dreamstime.com: Dan Rieck (bc); Seatraveler (tr). FLPA: Gianpiero Ferrari (br). 130–131 Alamy Stock Photo: Paul Strawson. 131 Alamy Stock Photo: AGF Srl (bl). 132 FLPA: Hugh Lansdown. Getty Images: Jim Abernethy (bl). 133 FLPA: Hugh Lansdown (l, r). 134 Press Association Images: Peter Morrison / AP (bl). 134–135 Martin Le-May. 136 FLPA: Kelvin Aitken / Biosphoto (bl). 136–137 OceanwideImages.com: Rudie Kuiter. 138 Dreamstime.com: Siraanamwong (bc). 138–139 Science Photo Library: Christopher Swann. 139 Alamy Stock Photo: WaterFrame (bl). 140 Corbis: Larry Madin / WHOI / Visuals Unlimited (b). 141 Corbis: Wim van Egmond / Visuals Unlimited (tl). FLPA:

Norbert Wu / Minden Pictures (br). Science Photo Library: Dante Fenolio (cl). 142–143 National News and Pictures / National News Press Agency: Ken Rotberg Photography. 144–145 Corbis: Mark Tomalty / Aurora Photos. 144 SuperStock: Prisma (bl). 146–147 Getty Images / iStock: RadimekCZ. 147 Dreamstime.com: Sean Pavone (cr). 148–149 Press Association Images: Jad Saab / AP. 149 Alamy Stock Photo: John Warburton-Lee Photography (tr). 150–151 Alamy Stock Photo: imageBROKER. 150 Dreamstime.com: John Takai (bl). 151 Alamy Stock Photo: Sergei Krestinin (bl). Corbis: Tourism Ministry / Xinhua Press (cr). Dreamstime.com: Andrei Tarchyshnik (bl). 152–153 Stephen Locke. 153 Alamy Stock Photo: Thierry Grun (cr). 154 Corbis: Mike Theiss / Ultimate Chase (cl). 154–155 Corbis: Reuters (t); Wave (b). 155 Corbis: Eric Nguyen (tr). Press Association Images: Stephen B. Thornton / AP (br). 156 Corbis: Mark Thiessen / National Geographic Creative. 156–157 Getty Images: Photographer's Choice. 158–159 Science Photo Library: NASA. 158 NASA: ESA / J.T. Trauger (Jet Propulsion Laboratory) (bl). 160–161 Stephan Kenzelmann. 160 NASA: JPL-Caltech / SETI Institute (bl). 162 Alamy Stock Photo: blickwinkel (b). Getty Images: Thomas Marent (cl). 163 Corbis: Tatyana Zenkovich / epa (br). Getty Images: Photolibrary (t). 164–165 Alamy Stock Photo: Navapon Plodprong. 165 Corbis: CJ Gunther / epa (tr). 166–167 Mick Petroff. 168–169 Corbis: Gerald & Buff Corsi / Visuals Unlimited. 168 National Geographic Creative: George Steinmetz (bl). 170 Alamy Stock Photo: Triangle Travels (cl). 170–171 Barcroft Media Ltd.: Janae Copelin

All other images © Dorling Kindersley